START & RUN AN INTERNET RESEARCH BUSINESS

Gerhard W. Kautz

Self-Counsel Press
(a division of)
International Self-Counsel Press Ltd.
USA   Canada

Self-Counsel Press acknowledges the financial support of the Government of Canada through the Book Publishing Industry Development Program (BPIDP) for our publishing activities.

Printed in Canada.

First edition: 2009

Library and Archives Canada Cataloguing in Publication

Kautz, Gerhard, 1938-
   Start & run an internet research business / Gerhard W. Kautz.

   ISBN 978-1-55180-836-9
   1. Internet research. 2. New business enterprises—Management.
   I. Title. II. Title: Start and run an internet research business.
   ZA4228.K73 2008   001.40285'4678   C2008-906242-6

Self-Counsel Press
(a division of)
International Self-Counsel Press Ltd.

1704 North State Street	1481 Charlotte Road
Bellingham, WA 98225	North Vancouver, BC V7J 1H1
USA	Canada

CONTENTS

ACKNOWLEDGMENTS

I would like to thank Cammie Ritchie and Terry Parr for their assistance in reviewing this book at the early stages, and providing many constructive comments that were incorporated into the book. I would also like to thank substantive editor Tanya Howe for her detailed review of the contents. Her wise requests for changes and additional explanations are much appreciated, as is her work at reformatting the book. Finally, I must thank the Self-Counsel Press staff for their encouragement to write the book, and more importantly, for their efforts to get it published.

— Gerhard W. Kautz

NOTICE TO READERS

The author, the publisher, and the vendor of this book make no representations or warranties regarding the outcome or the use to which the information in this book is put and are not assuming any liability for any claims, losses, or damages arising out of the use of this book. The reader should not rely on the author or publisher of this book for any professional advice.

INTRODUCTION

I have been running an Internet research business for about ten years, since I officially retired. It has been financially rewarding, but more importantly, it has been a lot of fun. I do almost all of my work from my home office, and I do the work when I want to. In effect, I am being paid to surf the net to keep up-to-date on the technological developments in my specialty, even though I am technically out of the workplace. This in itself is a huge reward. Another reward is the knowledge that I am helping both large and small companies.

This book is intended to help you start and run an Internet research business of your own. You may not know what you want to specialize in at this time, but this book will guide you through a decision-making process that should point you in the right direction. This book covers all of the aspects required for any business, but is aimed specifically at the Internet research business. You will learn about setting up your company, pricing your services, marketing, and getting contracts. The all-important matter of how to do the work is covered, as is the sometimes annoying work associated with the company administration.

Practical examples of Internet research businesses are used throughout the book to illustrate the instructions given. In addition, there are several samples and appendixes that contain examples and templates that you can adapt to your business. These samples as well as blank useable forms are included on the CD that comes with this book, along with Resources, which includes Internet search sites that you may need to do your research.

THE INTERNET RESEARCH BUSINESS AND YOU

1. The Internet Research Business

The Internet research business involves finding specific information on the Internet, for a client, and getting paid to do so. It also involves arranging and presenting the information in a form that is useful to the client, thus saving him or her considerable time. Occasionally, there will be a requirement to search other sources for information as well; however, most of the information will come from the Internet.

Companies around the world depend on information to stay in business and prosper. They need information on new technology, components for manufacturing, software, markets, competition — the list is almost endless. Companies have to find and evaluate the information, but this can be time consuming and costly for them. Internet research consultants can be hired to do this work for the companies much more cost-effectively than if the companies did the work themselves.

Who are these Internet research consultants? They are often one-person operations, working from their homes, in a specific information area. These people have usually, through previous employment,

An inexperienced searcher stands a chance of overlooking vital information, or worse, obtaining false information.

acquired specialized knowledge in a particular field. More importantly, they know where to go to get more and updated information for their clients. Of course, their main source of information is the Internet, but they do not limit their investigation to just using keywords and search engines. To validate the information and obtain more details, they also look in places such as relevant online magazine articles, company product lists, company annual reports, and press releases. They will search anywhere that will provide them with the detailed information that their clients have requested. This is the type of business that this book will help you get started and run.

2. How Companies Find Essential Information

Some companies subscribe to specialist information services that keep them up-to-date on their particular information requirements, but in most situations the companies get the information themselves. Larger companies may have a dedicated research department to provide the information for them; however, this can be a heavy expense on the company and certainly not one that can be afforded by most companies. Usually the people within the company who require information are forced to find it themselves. This is a very time consuming effort because these people are not experienced information miners. They usually just punch some keywords into an Internet search engine and use what comes up.

The Internet search method is very popular, but there can be some negative consequences. For example, an inexperienced searcher stands a chance of overlooking vital information, or worse, obtaining false information. However, the big negative is the time the employee spends looking for the information. This is time that should be devoted to profitable company-assigned tasks. It can cost the company dearly, particularly if, for example, a high-priced engineer spends days searching to see how other companies solved a particular design issue. This is where a contracted information researcher can save the company money by acquiring the information cost-effectively, and freeing the company employees to do their primary job functions.

The information required by companies varies with the company and within the company. Manufacturing companies rely heavily on information to improve their products, increase their productivity, and market their products profitably. The service industry needs information for the same reasons. The government requires a wide range of information. The type of information required by these potential customers is briefly discussed in the following sections. As you read through the sections, think about how you could help in obtaining the information for them. You may also be stimulated to consider other areas for which you could provide an effective information research service.

2.1 Manufacturing industry information research needs

Manufacturing companies rely heavily on information that is usually obtained by the employees who need it. A much more cost-effective source of information for them is an Internet research consultant, hired for a specific task, or on an annual contract. These companies need information to help them to —

- design the goods they will manufacture,
- develop the goods to manufacturing state,
- establish production methods,
- find the best sources of component supply,
- identify the market they should address,
- assess the competition,
- establish prices,
- determine the best sales methods,
- determine the best distribution methods, and
- obtain customer feedback.

As an Internet research consultant with knowledge and experience in one or more of the listed activities, you may be able to save the company considerable time and money by acquiring the required information for them, verifying it, and presenting it to them in easily usable form.

2.2 Service industry information research needs

The service industry also needs information. The obvious service companies with a need for information are the information companies themselves, but these companies already have trained staff to do the research work. In effect, they are your competition, but with much higher overheads. Some of the other service industry segments that can use the services of Internet research consultants are as follows.

2.2a Investment firms

Investment firms often have their own researchers to assess the viability of individual stocks and other investments, but may require additional research service for some of their projects.

2.2b Information technology companies

Information technology companies must keep up-to-date on the latest technological developments around the world and usually need help in doing so.

2.2c Lawyers

Lawyers need information to support and defend trials, lawsuits, divorces, etc.

2.2d Engineering and architecture firms

Engineers and architects must also keep up-to-date on the latest technological developments around the world and usually need help in doing so.

2.2e Business and trade organizations

Business and trade organizations are made up of companies with something in common, such as the defense industries or forestry companies. They often do research projects for their members and they usually contract out some or all of this work.

2.2f Individuals needing information

Individuals who need information could include almost anyone. Some examples include inventors who need help in patent searches, people considering starting a business but who need more information about it, or people working on family histories.

2.3 Government information research needs

The three levels of government require considerable information, but usually rely on their own staff to obtain it. They do occasionally contract out for help in this area, but the contracting process can be long and very documentation intensive. Many small companies do not bother with pursuing government business because they cannot afford the time and effort it takes to get the work.

3. Your Internet Research Business

Now that you understand the need companies have for information, the question is, "Why should they hire you to do the work?" The answer is simple — it costs them less if you do it. However, your biggest challenge will be to convince them of this fact, and that is where this book will help you.

It will take you through a process to evaluate your personal skills, experience, and knowledge that will help you select the area of expertise you should concentrate on in your Internet research business. You will then be shown how to develop a business model for your business; that is, what you will actually do to get business and make money. From the business model you can decide on the company structure you need and calculate some preliminary pricing. Good marketing and sales skills are the keys to any successful business and this book will help you with these important aspects. This book will guide you through your development of the process or processes you will use to actually do the work you are contracted for — efficiently. You will then be shown how to put all of this information together in a business plan. A business plan is a must for any business, for a number of reasons such as the following:

- It will make you consider problems before you encounter them in real life.
- It will indicate if you can make money with the business, and how much.
- It will help you predict your cash flow and help you decide if you need additional financing.
- It will explain the business and opportunity to those from whom you seek financing.
- It will generally keep you focused on the business, rather than allow you to go in several different directions.

The various concepts and issues covered in this book are explained with the use of examples of different Internet research businesses. A series of samples provide documents and tables that you can adapt to your own Internet research business. This book also covers the boring but necessary administrative chores such as bookkeeping and income tax.

As you read and work though this book, you should be in a position to set up and run a profitable Internet research business. The business will not only be very rewarding for you, but a lot of fun as well. In effect, you will be getting paid to surf the Net.

CHOOSING YOUR SPECIALIZATION

1. Why You Have to Specialize

There are several reasons why you have to specialize in one specific area of the Internet research business. The main reason is to utilize your personal experience and thus avoid a potentially steep learning curve. This chapter will help you analyze your experience, and direct you toward the specialty you should consider.

There are many other reasons to specialize that you will discover as you develop your business. For example, you will become more experienced in researching in a specific area and be able to identify relevant websites. You will also become more experienced at marketing your service to clients in your specialized area.

Having a specialized area will enable you to focus your marketing. You will have to market yourself, and it will be much more effective if it is focused. Chapters 6 and 7 will help you develop your marketing strategy and do the actual marketing.

2. Assess Your Skill Set

Before you begin identifying your area of specialization in the Internet research business, you should first determine if you have the skills to carry out the business. You have the basic skills of being able to read and make logical decisions. However, you will need some additional skills to have a successful Internet research business. These are discussed in the following sections.

2.1 Computer skill

It is pretty obvious that to do research on the Internet you have to have at least some computer skill. You do not have to be a computer whiz, and you certainly do not have to know the technical aspects of a computer. All you need is the basic skill to use a computer as a tool, and know how to access the Internet.

2.2 Communication skills

Good communication skills are essential in running any successful business; not necessarily to do the work, but to get the contracts and understand clients' needs. Written communication skills are required to make the initial contact with potential clients, and to deliver the final product in the form of a written report.

Listening skills are required to understand what the client is asking you to do. You will often have to augment this with perception skills to fully understand what the client wants, even though he or she is not being clear in his or her request. The skill of knowing how to ask the right questions is also important for understanding the client's wishes.

2.3 Investigative skills

You should also have basic investigative skills to do the work. For example, as you are going through a company's annual report to assess it as a competitor to your client, and you see that the company has just purchased a smaller company, you should investigate the smaller company as well. However, you must be able to curb your investigative curiosity to avoid going off in a direction that will only waste your time.

2.4 Personal skill assessment

If you are weak in any of the previously mentioned skills, you should do something to improve your skill set. For example, if you are worried about not being good enough on the computer to be successful, a basic community-run course on how to work the Internet may be all you need. Or, maybe reading a book on the subject would help improve your skills.

If you think you have all the necessary skills, then you have the basics needed to start and run an Internet research business.

3. Assess Your Experience

Your personal experience will probably determine the area in which you should direct your Internet research business. To do the assessment, consider the experience you gained over the years, particularly in the following categories.

3.1 Work Experience

It is assumed that most people reading this book have had work experience, and some people may be close to retirement with considerable work experience. That experience may have been limited to a few particular areas or it could involve a variety of previous jobs. Either way, you will have gained experience that may be of value in an Internet research business.

To begin, create a list of your work experiences and as you think of more experiences add them to your list. You will be surprised at the variety of work experience you have had over the years. For example, your list may include:

- House construction
- Buying manufacturing components for a company
- Installing equipment for customers
- Sales in different areas

Make sure you list each sales experience separately by the products you sold, because the sales area may be significant in your assessment.

Next you want to rank these experiences in three categories —

- depth of experience you obtained,
- how good you were at doing the job, and
- how much you enjoyed doing the work.

Your personal experience will probably determine the area in which you should direct your Internet research business.

Your objective is to have three lists of the same experiences, but in different relative order, numbered with the highest experience being number one, and all others following in the order you determine. The ranking does not have to be precise, only a comparison of each item against the others. You will use these rankings to do an overall assessment of where you should specialize in your Internet research business.

For the depth of experience section, rank each item on your list by how much useful experience you obtained. If you gained a tremendous amount of practical experience in one area, this will probably be your number one ranking. Some experiences may have been only fleeting, and they of course will get a very low ranking. Using the example list of experiences above, you may have spent most of your time installing equipment for customers, so this will be your number one under depth of experience. The house construction may have just been a brief summer job years ago, so this will be at or near the bottom of your list. Similarly, your sales experience may have been part-time years ago, such as when you worked as a grocery checkout clerk. The other items will fall in between according to how you assess them relatively.

Next consider how good you were at each experience on your list. This is, of course, your opinion on how good you were, so make sure you do an honest assessment. Using the examples again, you may not have done well at installing equipment, even though you did it for quite a while, so this experience would be way down on your list. You may have done quite well at dealing with customers in your sales positions, so this would be higher on the list. You may also feel that you did a good job when dealing with suppliers when you were a buyer for a manufacturing company, so this goes high on the list.

Finally, assess each experience you had according to how much you enjoyed the work. You may not really have liked the face-to-face encounters with customers, but you did like talking to suppliers on the telephone. By far your happiest experience may have been during the construction job, when you dealt with tools and techniques that were all new to you. Arrange your list accordingly.

3.2 Hobby and sports experience

Hobbies can also lead to jobs or careers. Many people have been able to turn a passionate hobby into a lucrative business. You may think you do not have or have had a hobby that could lead to a business, but have you really considered it? Think of all the hobbies you had or attempted. List them in the order you would like to pursue them as a business, and put them in the evaluation table. The list could include, for example, woodworking, gardening, or photography.

Sports should also be considered, particularly if you are very active in one or more sports, such as organized soccer or baseball. Even if you are only a casual participant, such as a round of golf two or three times a year, list it. Then arrange the sports in your order of priority.

Put the hobby and sports lists together and arrange them in order of priority. Some hobbies may outrank some sports, and vice versa. Then put the list into the evaluation table suggested in Section **4**.

3.3 Educational experience

You may have more than one university degree, or you may have only a high school diploma. However, over the years you probably have taken many short courses such as on computer spreadsheets, yoga, beekeeping, or building a basement recreation room. List all of these in their order of importance.

4. Overall Personal Assessment

By now you may have already decided on an Internet research business specialty, or you may be starting to zero in on one. However, if you are still wondering, Table 1 will help you in your overall assessment. In it you make a listing of all your experiences, assessed in each category. In each column, the number one assessed item is at the top and the others follow below it in the priority you gave them. The examples shown in Table 1 are those mentioned in the previous paragraphs. Your lists may be shorter or longer than this example.

On the CD included with this book, you will find a blank version of the experience evaluation table ready for you to complete.

5. Select Your Specialization

The evaluation table you made should help you select your specialization. Take a look at the top row of items and see if anything pops out at you. In the examples used in this chapter, which are summarized in Table 1, the top row of experience items is installing equipment, company buyer, house construction, woodworking, and university arts degree. Installing equipment and university arts degree do not indicate an Internet research business specialty. However, company buyer, house construction, and woodworking deserve some serious consideration.

TABLE 1
EXPERIENCE EVALUATION

Work Experience *Depth*	Work Experience *Good At*	Work Experience *Enjoyed*	Hobby Experience	Educational Experience
Installing equipment	Company buyer	House construction	Woodworking	University arts degree
Other	Other	Company buyer	Baseball	Basement recreation room
Company buyer	House construction	Hardware store clerk	Other	Other
Other	Other	Other	Soccer	Computer spreadsheets
Hardware store clerk	Other	Other	Gardening	Other
Other	Hardware store clerk	Other	Other	Other
House construction	Other	Other	Other	Beekeeping
Other	Other	Other	Photography	Other
Other	Installing equipment	Installing equipment	Other	Yoga
Grocery store checkout	Grocery store checkout	Grocery store checkout	Golf	Other

If nothing comes from the first row, look at the second row of items, and let yourself explore these areas. Then explore the third row, and so on. You should be able to come up with a specialization, or some areas to consider further.

Again using the example, the second line has company buyer, baseball, and a basement recreation room construction course. Baseball is probably not a consideration, but company buyer is. More importantly, during the basement recreation room construction course, the instructor may have talked about several new products on the market that applied to house construction in general. So putting together company buyer, house construction, woodworking, and the new products associated with basement recreation room construction, a specialty could emerge. Home building and construction companies are always on the lookout for new products that will reduce their costs, and make the finished product more attractive to the home buyer. Why not specialize in researching new house construction products for home building and construction companies?

The evaluation process should help you select a specialty. In addition to the data you wrote down and analyzed, you will also have to apply some original thought. As the common saying goes, you might have to "think outside the box." This process is only a tool to help you focus your thoughts. It is up to you to identify your Internet research business specialization.

6. Changing Your Specialization

As your Internet research business progresses, you may find that your specialization is expanding, or that there is not enough business coming in with your selected specialization. If your specialization is expanding, and your business is as well, let it do so, as long as it makes business sense. However, if you find you are branching out into too many areas, and neglecting business opportunities associated with your defined core specialization, go back to that specialization because it is probably more cost-effective for you.

If you find that there is not enough business coming in with your chosen specialization, review your marketing and sales efforts. This is often the downfall of a business; insufficient or ineffective marketing and sales. You have to put a lot of time and effort into it to establish and continue business. Make sure you are doing so before you make any radical changes.

If you think you are doing adequate marketing and sales, but the business is just not there, you could be right to change your specialization. Review your business plan, particularly the sections on defining the business opportunity and determining what should be your market share. You will now have a better estimate of the numbers involved, which will enable you to redo your business plan. If the newly worked results confirm that there is not sufficient business in the specialization you have chosen, you obviously have to make some changes.

To change your specialization, go back and look at the work you did to make your initial selection. If you see some glaring omissions, add them to your experience evaluation table, and do a re-evaluation. Maybe this will lead to a specialization change. If there are no omissions, look at the second or third tier of options you may have in your experience evaluation table. If you see a possibility, write a new business plan based on it. If the results of the business planning are positive, go for it. Just remember, be flexible, but also be rational.

YOUR BUSINESS MODEL

1. What Is a Business Model?

Basically, the business model is how you will make money. There are many academic definitions and dissertations of the business model, but for your purpose, it is a model or procedure detailing how you will make money in the Internet research business. Do not confuse the business model with the business plan, which is covered in Chapter 12. The business plan contains elements of the business model, but it deals with a broader business perspective including how you will finance and grow your business.

You should develop a business model for a number of reasons. The main reason is to make you think about how you will actually do the business. Another reason is that as you write down the way you will work, you will probably think of more aspects of doing the business. Once you have developed your business model, and are working it, it will help you to stay focused on what you are doing.

The following sections explain what should go into your business model. Sample 1 at the end of this chapter contains a sample business model for a fictitious lawyer-background information service.

The examples used in each section of this chapter relate to the fictitious Sample 1 at the end of the chapter.

2. The Business Opportunity

Academics call this first step in the business model the *Value Proposition*. This is the area in which you define what you think might be the client's problem that he or she wants solved. Then you explain how you will solve the problem for him or her. You also want to identify what the value of your problem solution is to the client. This will confirm the viability of your business, and the points you identify here will also be useful in your marketing and sales.

Sample 1 at the end of this chapter contains a sample business model of an Internet research business that provides background information for court cases. The following is an example used from Sample 1.

Example

As a court reporter, Ms. B noticed that quite often lawyers needed background information on side issues of a case, such as what the weather was like on the day of the incident under trial, the statistical number of similar incidents that take place in the defendant's occupation, etc. The lawyers have to get this information from somewhere, and Ms. B figured she could do it for them very cost-effectively.

3. What Is Your Market?

You need to identify what or who your market is, where it is, and how big it is. First you have to carefully define who would want your services so you don't waste your time and resources going after the wrong companies or people. Client definition (defining your target market) is very important because it will be the basis for most of your other business activities, such as marketing. Be prepared to give it considerable thought.

Next you want to identify where your potential clients are. Are you going to target clients in your city, in several cities, or in the whole country? Your thought process will also have to involve the size of the market. You will want to cover a wide enough area to ensure you have sufficient potential clients, but you don't want to overdo it and bite off more than you can chew.

Here is where you use your Internet research skills to find the information you need for yourself. Using your defined description of your potential clients, find out how many of them there are in a particular area. For example, if you are targeting electronics manufacturing companies, do an Internet search for electronics manufacturers plus the initial area you are considering. As the various websites listing these companies come up, scrutinize them to make sure they are the ones you want, and start counting. Then expand your search as you require. Keep a record of the sites with the company information because you will need that information later for your marketing activities.

Your marketing procedure is probably the most important part of your business.

Example

Ms. B defined her potential clients simply as lawyers. She then did an Internet search for lawyers plus her city. Several sites came up, but the Yellow Pages site listed what appeared to be all of them. She simply counted those listed. She also went to the Internet site of the law society covering her jurisdiction, and estimated the number of lawyers listed there. She determined that her client base was somewhere around these two numbers.

4. Your Marketing Procedure

Marketing is the way you promote your business to prospective customers. You cannot have a successful business without some form of marketing. It can be anywhere from simple word of mouth to a series of television ads. Your marketing procedure is probably the most important part of your business. This is how you tell potential clients about your service and get them interested in it. Spend as much time as you can developing it. Chapters 6 and 7 lead you through the marketing process for your business.

Example

Ms. B determined that she could not rely on word-of-mouth promotion because of the nature of her business. She decided that the best way for her to tell potential clients about her service was by direct mail, with a convincing letter, and a handy reply form that clients could mail or fax back to her. She also had to start with a small number of lawyers, rather than target all of them in her city at once. (Her marketing procedure is shown in Sample 1.)

5. Your Sales Procedure

For the purpose of this book, "sales" is considered the activity of closing the deals and getting contracts. This happens once you have potential clients interested in your service. Your sales procedure is therefore as important as your marketing procedure. Both have to exist in a successful business. Chapter 8 discusses how to get the contracts, or sales procedures, that should work for your Internet research business.

Example

Ms. B realized there were several different ways of handling the sales procedure after a successful marketing contact with a potential client. It all depended on how the client responded to her marketing, and what she asked for. She also realized that she would have to move fast when that client response was made, so she decided to outline suitable answers to the various client responses. (Her sales procedure is shown in Sample 1.)

6. Your Project Work Procedure

Your project work procedure is the way in which you will do the work. It is also what many consider the fun part of the business. Chapter 11 goes through this aspect of the business in detail. You first have to verify that you understand what the client needs, and not necessarily just what he or she asked for. You then do the search using appropriate search engines and Internet sites, making sure the information you get is accurate. Finally, you have to write a report that will be the product you deliver to the client.

The work procedure in Sample 1, developed by Ms. B, is standard for any Internet research business. However, make sure you consider each aspect of it with regard to your business. Chapter 11 will help you do this.

7. Your Delivered Products

The main item to be delivered to the client is the report on your research findings, but you also want to include some other items. Of course you want to get paid, so you must include an invoice or bill. If there is a potential for follow-on work, you could also include a proposal to do it. You should always include a handy fax form or email template for the client to send to you for future information searches.

In Sample 1 you will find Ms. B's list of delivered products.

BUSINESS MODEL FOR MS. B'S LAWYER BACKGROUND INFORMATION SERVICE

1. Business Opportunity

The business opportunity is that for some cases lawyers need background information to prove or disprove some aspects of a case. If they try to get the information themselves, it will take them considerable time to do so. It is also probably not cost-effective for them to have a full-time researcher on their staff to do this work.

The solution to the lawyers' problem is to be able to call Ms. B's service and have her find the information for them.

The value of this problem solution to the lawyer clients is that —

- they get the required information much quicker because Ms. B knows where to go to get it; and

- the cost of getting the information is much less because Ms. B's rates are less than the lawyer's, and she will take considerable less time to get the information.

The business would aim at long-term relationships with clients, possibly even with annual contracts or retainers.

2. The Market

The number of lawyers listed in the city *Yellow Pages* is 490. The Law Society lists about 500 lawyers in the city. Therefore, if the market area is only the city, the potential clients number about 500.

3. Marketing Procedure

The marketing procedure to potential clients would be as follows:

- Identify potential lawyer clients to target from various databases including:

  - *Yellow Pages*

  - Bar associations lists

- Investigate each lawyer via his or her website or other documentation to establish that he or she is a suitable client prospect who needs information research.

- Obtain the client's interest through direct-mail advertising to him or her, either by email or by postal mail. Include a form for the client to complete and fax back, requesting further information, a meeting or telephone call, a sample contract, or a specific information search. Also invite the potential client to request more information by telephone or email.

4. Sales Procedure

The sales procedure to obtain a contract or purchase order from the client is as follows:

- If the potential client returns a completed fax form requesting further information, call him or her and give the client a prepared sales pitch as soon as possible.

- If the client requests a meeting or telephone call, arrange it as soon as possible.
- If the client requests a sample contract, send him or her a one-year contract outlining what Ms. B will do, how the client is to task her, her deliverables, and her hourly rates.
- If the client requests a proposal for a specific information search, send it to him or her including a not-to-exceed price and a suggested contracting procedure.
- In a few weeks, always follow up the initial response made to a potential client.

5.   Project Work Procedure

The procedure to carry out the project work for each contracted project is as follows:

- Verify the client's needs to ensure full understanding of not only the client's request, but his or her needs as well.
- Establish keywords or phrases to begin the information search. These will probably change as the project proceeds.
- Begin the search using a standard search engine such as Google.
- As relevant information is obtained, begin drafting the report. This will help identify what additional information searching is required.
- Confirm each information item via another source.
- Reference each information item with its source.
- Draft a synopsis of the relevant information aimed at the client's needs that he or she can quickly scan, and if the client needs more information, he or she can refer to the detailed findings of the search.
- Draft the final report to the client.

6.   Delivered Products

The main delivered product would be a report detailing the information the customer requested, including the following:

- A synopsis of the relevant information aimed at the client's needs that he or she can quickly scan, and if the client needs more information, he or she can refer to the detailed findings of the search.
- The agreed search mandate and parameters.
- The areas that were covered, if applicable.
- Detailed findings of the search, and the references where the information came from.

The delivered package to the customer should also include the following:

- The billing invoice in a standard form.
- A cover letter that talks about the report, the invoice, and makes recommendations for further work, if applicable.
- A fax form and/or email template for future information searches.

YOUR COMPANY STRUCTURE

1. Why You Need a Company

The main reason to create a company is for income tax purposes. You will have to pay income tax on the money you earn, and you do this through some form of company structure. However, creating a company also allows you to claim expenses against your income, and thus reduce your income tax. (Chapter 5, section **2.**, discusses overhead cost factors and lists some of the items you may want to consider as expenses in your business.)

Another reason for a company structure is to make yourself look more professional. You can also make it look like you are a much larger company than just yourself. This can be important to some clients until they get to know you.

You therefore have to decide on the best company structure for you. This will depend on the laws in your particular state or province, and you may want to speak to your accountant and/or lawyer about what is best for you. The following are some of the issues you should consider in setting up your company:

➭ Will you have employees?

- How big do you think your company will grow?
- Are lawsuits possible?
- How easily do you want to draw cash out of the business?
- What is the best tax structure?
- How much will it cost to set up the company?

There are a number of different company structures you can set up. Each one has its own advantages and disadvantages. You will have to choose the one which suits your requirements and circumstances. The following sections briefly describe the different types of company structures, along with their advantages and disadvantages. These are general descriptions, and there may be variations or differences in your state or province. Much of the information in this chapter comes from the following sites that you can visit for more details. The links for these sites are included on the CD in the Resources section.

- USA Government Small Business Administration (SBA)
- United States Department of the Treasury / Internal Revenue Service
- Government of Canada, Forms of Business Organization

2. Incorporated Company

The incorporated company is a legal entity that is separate from its shareholding owners. A corporation can be taxed, it can be sued, and it can enter into contractual agreements. The shareholders are not personally liable for the actions of the company, including the debts.

The shareholders elect a board of directors to oversee the major policies and decisions. The corporation has a life of its own and does not dissolve when ownership changes.

The cost of incorporation varies, but it generally costs around $1,000 to register it. You will also have legal fees that will add another $1,000 or more to the cost.

In the USA, corporations are registered and controlled by the state. In Canada, they can be either provincially or federally registered. In general there are two kinds of corporations:

- A *private corporation* can be formed by one or more people. It cannot sell shares or securities to the general public.

- A *public corporation* issues securities (shares) for public distribution. It has considerably more reporting requirements.

The advantages of a corporation include:

- Shareholders have limited liability for the corporation's debts or lawsuits against the corporation.

- Generally, shareholders can only be held accountable for their investment in stock of the company. (Note however, that officers can be held personally liable for their actions.)

- Corporations can raise additional funds through the sale of stock.

The disadvantages of a corporation include:

- The process of incorporation requires more time and money than other forms of company structure.

- Corporations are monitored by federal, state, or province, and some local agencies. As a result, they have more paperwork to comply with regulations.

- Incorporating may result in higher overall taxes. Dividends paid to shareholders are not deductible from business income, thus you can be taxed twice.

3. Partnership

A partnership is a business owned by two or more people. Legally, the owners are just as liable as the business itself. The partners, or owners, must also agree on a number of issues associated with the partnership. A partnership agreement should be drawn up with the aid of an attorney that details how these issues will be shared or resolved, such as the following:

- How much money each partner will contribute to the partnership.

- How much time each partner will contribute to the partnership.

- How the profits will be shared.

- How decisions will be made.

- How disputes will be resolved.

- How future partners will be admitted to the partnership.

- What the procedure is to buy out partners.
- What steps will be taken to dissolve the partnership when the time comes to do so.

Advantages of a partnership include:

- Partnerships are relatively easy to set up.
- With more than one owner, the ability to raise funds may be increased.
- The profits from the business flow directly through to the partners' personal tax returns.
- Prospective employees may be attracted to the business if given the incentive to become a partner.
- The business usually will benefit from partners who have complementary skills.

Disadvantages of a partnership include:

- Partners are jointly and individually liable for the actions of the other partners.
- Profits must be shared with others.
- Disagreements can occur.

4. Limited Liability Corporation (LLC)

The LLC is a relatively new type of hybrid business structure in the USA, which is now permissible in most states. It provides the limited liability features of a corporation and the tax efficiencies and operational flexibility of a partnership. The owners are members, and the duration of the LLC is limited but can be changed. Formation of the LLC is more complex and formal than that of a general partnership.

For more information about LLCs, see *How to Form and Operate a Limited Liability Company*, another book from Self-Counsel Press (for US readers).

5. Sole Proprietorship

Sole proprietorships are the simplest way to set up a business. In this case, the business is owned by one person, the sole proprietor, who owns all the assets of the business and any profits generated. This sole proprietor is also fully responsible for all debts and obligations related to the business. A creditor with a claim against a sole proprietor has a right against all of the owner's assets, whether business or personal. This is known as unlimited liability. Registration requirements vary from state to state and province to province, but generally the process is relatively simple and inexpensive.

Advantages of a sole proprietorship include:

- ➡ It's the easiest and least expensive form of ownership to organize.
- ➡ Sole proprietors are in complete control of the business.
- ➡ Sole proprietors receive all income generated by the business.
- ➡ Profits from the business flow directly to the owner's personal income tax return.
- ➡ The business is easy to dissolve when the time comes to do so.

Disadvantages of a sole proprietorship include:

- ➡ Sole proprietors have unlimited liability and are legally responsible for all debts against the business. Their business and personal assets are at risk.
- ➡ Raising funds may be a problem.

Initially, the recommended business structure for your Internet research business is a sole proprietorship.

6. Recommended Company Structure

In the Internet research business you should not have too many concerns about being sued by a client. So the main advantage of a corporation, the limited liability, is not a factor for you. Also, the cost and effort of setting up a corporation is probably not worth it for your business.

If you are thinking of going into business with someone else, you may want to investigate a partnership structure. But if it is just you, you definitely do not need to go through the process of setting up a partnership.

This brings us to the sole proprietorship. As a one-person business, you should probably start with this structure. If your business grows, and you want to incorporate or team with somebody and create a partnership, you can do that later. But initially, the recommended business structure for your Internet research business is a sole proprietorship.

PRICING

1. Price Quotations

Pricing is a very important part of your Internet research business. It determines how much money you are going to make, and also affects how much business you will get. If you price yourself too high, you will get very little business, if any, and thus make little or no money. If you price yourself too low, you may have lots of business, but you could be making more money. So you have to establish a price for your services that is good for you. You might even want to set a price range, because you may decide to charge different clients different rates.

Potential clients will always want to know the price of your services. In some cases you will quote an overall project price to them, and in other cases you will quote an hourly rate because you and the client do not know exactly how much work will be involved. Also, if you get annual contracts, the hourly rate will have to be stated in the contract. (For an annual contract you may want to give the client a lower rate than for a one-time project, and this is why you may want to consider establishing a price range.)

2. Overhead Cost Factors

The first thing you need to do to set your price rate is to work out your overhead costs. You probably will not get this right the first time, and you will probably change some numbers after you work out your first year's expenses for your income tax. However, you have to come up with some estimates now because they will determine your pricing.

Work out your overhead costs on an annual basis. Each person's situation is a little different and costs will vary accordingly. The following list includes some costs for you to consider:

- Home office usage: You probably will not rent an office to start with, but you will use a spare room in your home, a corner of the basement, or even your kitchen table. There is a legitimate cost associated with this. For example, if you use a spare room in the house, you can assign a percentage of the household costs to your business. The percentage may be based on the square footage of the room compared to the overall house square footage, or if it is one of six rooms, you can simply say it takes up one sixth or 17 percent of the household costs. The following list includes household costs:

  - Rent or mortgage interest

  - Insurance

  - Taxes

  - Heating

  - Electricity

  - Telephone (if you do not have a company line)

  - Water

  - Maintenance

  - Security (if you pay for a service)

  - Cleaning (if you pay for a service)

  - Office supplies: You will need all of the standard items you have in an office, and you will have to buy them yourself for your company. Some of the office supplies will include:

    - Printer paper

    - Printer cartridges

- Company stationery such as business cards, letterhead, envelopes
- Storage boxes
- Desk tools such as staplers, hole punches

⊟ Telephone: You may want to have a separate company line in your house. You may even need two lines — one for the telephone and another for the fax. Some telephone companies offer these two services on one incoming line, but with two telephone numbers. The second telephone can be connected to the fax and it can be distinguished by two quick rings while the other line has the normal telephone ring.

⊟ Cell phone: You may just use an ordinary cell phone, or go with more capability such as the BlackBerry® or equivalent messaging system.

⊟ Postage and courier.

⊟ Office furniture: Usually you charge a percentage, perhaps 20 percent, each year as depreciation.

⊟ Computer and peripherals: These are usually depreciated on an annual basis, but at a higher rate such as 30 percent.

⊟ Software.

⊟ Internet service.

⊟ Website: As explained in Chapter 7, there are a number of expenses associated with having a website. These include the monthly or annual hosting charges, the annual registration charges, as well as the developing and maintenance charges.

⊟ Research material: You will sometimes have to do research through sources other than the Internet, such as in a book on a particular subject that you will have to purchase. Also, to keep up-to-date in your specialization you may subscribe to certain magazines or newspapers. These are part of your cost of doing business.

⊟ Transportation: The main cost in this category will be your vehicle, especially now with vehicle costs running in excess of 60 cents a mile, or 40 cents a kilometer.

⊟ Advertising and promotion: You may not spend much, if any, on advertising. However, you will spend money on promotion,

Your billable time will probably be very low at the start of your business, as you struggle to get clients.

such as taking clients to lunch or sending them season's greetings. These are all business expenses, but sometimes only a portion can be claimed as income tax deductions.

- ⊟ Miscellaneous: There will be unanticipated expenses that do not fall into any of the above categories. At this stage, just take an estimate of what these expenses will be.

3. Salary Expectations

Next you have to establish how much money you expect to make. You can base this on the annual salary you made in your last job or on what you would like to make. If you use your previous salary, don't forget to add something for unpaid company benefits such as health insurance. But don't be greedy. Make your expectation realistic, because you do not want to price yourself out of the market.

4. Billable Time, Company Time, and Personal Time

Billable time is time you actually spend on a project, for which you can charge a client. Company time is time you spend doing work associated with your company that you cannot charge against a project or client. You will have to set up a system to keep track of both of these on a daily basis, as described in Chapter 13. Personal time is just that — time for holidays, sick days, or time off.

Your billable time will probably be very low at the start of your business, as you struggle to get clients. Hopefully the business will pick up and you will arrive at the happy state in which you are working on client paid projects most of your time. You should use this future percentage of billable time to establish your pricing, and at this stage you will have to estimate it. It would be great if your billable time was four out of five days a week, but in all likelihood it will be less.

Company time will be high at first as you sort out your administration procedures and generally get organized. You will also have to devote considerable time to promoting yourself to clients. Even initial marketing visits to potential clients cannot be billed, and so it must be counted as company time. In the first year you can count on spending a lot of your time and effort on company time, but it should reduce as your business gets going. Again, it is the company time you spend later on that you should use in your pricing calculations.

Example

As Mr. A was setting up his Internet research business, he visualized what he thought would be his future time allotments. He did his estimates for the three categories of time as follows:

Personal time:

He allowed for three weeks holiday each year, or 15 working days. He would also take off statutory holiday Mondays, Christmas, New Years, etc. These would total about 10 days a year. He estimated he would have to take off 10 sick days on average during the year. His total personal time for the year would be 35 days.

Company time:

He figured he would have to spend about one day a week promoting his business to get clients. In a 52-week year this would be 52 days. He also allowed a half day per week for administrative activities, or 26 days a year. Thus the total company time would be 78 days annually.

Billable time:

The maximum amount of billable time he could have would be the time available in the year less the allowed personal time and company time. With five "working" days per week, and 52 weeks per year, the available days are 260 annually. Subtracting from this the 35 personal days and the 78 company days, the maximum billable days he could have was 147 annually.

5. Markup Factors

Once you have calculated a basic charge-out rate or price for your time, like all for-profit companies, you may want to mark it up to allow for other factors. Companies usually do markups on a percentage basis.

5.1 Specialization

If you are offering a highly specialized and useful service that will save the clients time and money, you may want to add something to the basic price you calculated because demand for your service will be high. This could vary from a few percentage points to 10 percent or more, depending on how specialized or salable you or your company is.

5.2 Competition

Competition can affect your pricing. If there is little or no competition, you could take a chance and mark up your rates. If there is competition, you may actually have to reduce your price in order to get contracts.

5.3 Client understanding of personnel costs

You will run across some clients who will be shocked at your price because they do not fully understand the price of labor. Others, particularly in the service industry, will mentally relate your hourly rate with their own charge-out rates. Their rates could be very high, such as lawyers, or engineering companies, so if your rates are a fraction of theirs, they will not quibble with you. You may want to mark up your rates slightly higher for these clients.

5.4 Profit

Since you are a for-profit company, you may want to add a small percentage to your calculated price or rate, for profit. For example, 10 percent or 15 percent is very reasonable.

6. Overall Pricing Approach

Having considered all of the previously mentioned pricing issues, you can now calculate an official price or charge-out rate for your services. You should work it out for an hour's service, although sometimes clients may want you to quote to them on the basis of an eight-hour day. The best way to explain the overall pricing process is with the following example.

> *Example*
>
> *Mr. A went through the process of establishing his price.*
>
> *Overhead:*
>
> *He totaled his annual house costs, which came to $34,268. Since he would use the spare bedroom in his seven-room home as an office, he calculated one seventh of the amount as his office "rental" cost. This came to $4,895. He then worked through the list of other overhead costs, using utility bills and the like to establish the costs. For some he just had to make an estimate of the annual cost. The cost of these other items came*

to $4,977. His total annual overhead would be (4,895 + 4,977) $9,872.

Salary expectation:

In his last job he was earning about $58,000 a year, plus company benefits. He added $12,000 for the company benefits, and so his salary expectation was $70,000 per year.

Time calculation:

Mr. A's time calculations are in the example in Section 4. He had arrived at the maximum billable days per year of 147.

Basic price calculation:

With his total overhead of $9,872, and his salary expectation of $70,000, his basic annual company income would have to be $79,872. This equated to (79,872 ÷ 147) $543.35 per eight-hour day, or about $67.92 per hour.

Markup:

Mr. A did not think his specialty warranted any extra markup. He did not know of any competition in his area, so he decided not to add or subtract anything for it in the beginning. Client understanding markup would depend on the situations as he encountered them. However, he did decide on a small 10 percent profit markup, or about $6.79.

Final price:

When he added the 10 percent profit to the base price he had calculated, it came out to (6.79 + 67.92) $74.71 per hour. He decided that his price, or charge-out rate would be $75 per hour.

CHAPTER 6

MARKETING

1. Why You Must Market

Marketing is how you tell your potential clients about your service. You have to market in some form or you will not get any business. It can range from simple word-of-mouth marketing, where you and your friends tell potential clients about your service, to full-blown media advertising involving television commercials. Your marketing will be in between these two extremes.

Always remember, you have to market your service to stay in business. Even if you are swamped with work, you still have to market for future work, because today's projects will come to an end and have to be replaced with new projects.

This chapter will help you develop your marketing strategy and methods. This chapter will also help you think through each aspect of your marketing approach, and help you ensure cost-effective marketing. (Chapter 7 will help you develop the marketing material.)

2. Define Potential Clients

Before you start marketing, you have to define who your potential clients are so you can target them effectively. You cannot just say, "I am going to market to the high-tech industry or the construction industry." You have to be more specific or you will waste a lot of effort targeting the wrong market.

Your client definition will of course depend on your Internet research specialty. You don't have to be too specific in your definition. For example, you can go after large or small companies in a particular industrial sector, or companies that are involved in one specific product. The following example will illustrate how you can narrow down your potential client definition to the right ones.

Example

Ms. B, from Sample 1, in Chapter 3, had defined her potential clients as lawyers in her city. However, the list was far too large for her to start marketing to, so she decided to try to single out those lawyers who would need her service. She Googled "lawyer specialty" and got a number of sites that listed various legal specialties. One in particular was very useful in that it listed about 30 specialties and gave a brief description of each. The list ranged from adoption lawyers to environmental lawyers, to lawyers specializing in wills.

Since Ms. B's Internet research business would be for background information on nonlegal aspects of court cases, she quickly realized that many of the specialties would not be interested in her service. Going through the list and definitions, she came up with those that would need nonlegal background information in some of their cases. These specialties for her were: criminal lawyers, intellectual property lawyers, litigation lawyers, medical malpractice lawyers, and personal injury lawyers. These were the types of lawyers to whom she would market her services.

3. Identify and Select Potential Clients

Once you have defined your potential clients you can then look for them. The Internet, of course, will help you do this. Google the keywords of what you are looking for, for example, radio manufacturers. Many sites will come up, but the ones that will help you the most are those that are relevant associations that list their member companies. The lists usually have a link to the member company's website. Have a quick scan of the company site and determine if this is a potential customer for you. If it is a potential customer, save the company's contact information because you will need it later.

4. Assess Marketing Methods

Once you have defined your marketing targets, you then have to decide which marketing methods you will use. For your small company, cost will be an issue, so you want to get the most you can from your small budget. The following sections describe some of the marketing methods you should consider.

4.1 Slogan

You should have a short but very descriptive slogan for your business that you can put on your business card, stationery, and website. It should describe your business in a way that gets the potential clients' interest. For example, *Helping You Keep Up With Technology.*

4.2 Business cards

You have to have suitable business cards to give to potential clients, and to pass around in general. Chapter 7, section **2.**, describes some of the things you should consider when creating your business card.

4.3 Word of mouth

Word of mouth is simply passing information about you and your business verbally, to friends and contacts. This is the most basic form of marketing, but is somewhat limited.

4.4 Networking

Networking is taking the word-of-mouth approach a step higher, by attending gatherings where you can meet potential clients and pitch your business to them. The gatherings can range from cocktail parties, to community organization meetings, to business organization meetings.

4.5 Business organizations

It may be worth considering joining one or more business organizations that are associated with the type of Internet research you do. However, the annual fees can be expensive, and you may want to hold off on this until your business is more established.

4.6 Website

You have to have a website, to which you can refer potential clients. If you can get it situated high up on search engines, it can also be a

It may be worth considering joining one or more business organizations that are associated with the type of Internet research you do.

very powerful business magnet. Chapter 7, section **4.**, describes some of the things you should consider in your website.

4.7 Trade show participation

These days there are trade shows for everything, and it is difficult to identify which ones can bring you new business. Trade shows are also expensive to participate in, so before you commit to one check it out by just attending it.

4.8 Trade show milking

Rather than participate in a trade show, simply attend it and pass out your brochures to potential clients in their booths.

4.9 Media advertising

Media advertising is very expensive, and probably not too effective for most Internet research businesses. However, there might be appropriate trade magazines in which you could place a small ad that would be seen by potential clients.

4.10 Telephone soliciting

Nobody likes this — neither the caller nor the called. However, if you know the potential client, or just know his or her telephone number, it could be worth a try. But be prepared for a cold shoulder, and have some good opening statements to get the person's attention.

4.11 Direct-postal-mail advertising

Direct-postal-mail advertising involves sending an introductory marketing letter and/or brochure to the potential clients you have identified. Include in your mail package a form or other way for the potential client to easily get back to you for more information. You may have to do more than one mailing to each potential client to get attention. Chapter 7 discusses marketing letters, brochures, and client response forms.

4.12 Direct-email advertising

Direct-email advertising is as annoying to the receiver as telephone soliciting, so use it sparingly. If you do use it, treat it the same way as direct postal mail. Do not put your letter or brochure as an attachment, but put it in the body of your email. You should also be aware of some recent laws that put restrictions on email solicitation. (See Chapter 7, section **8.**, for more information about unsolicited email.)

5. Marketing Time Line

Once you have decided on your marketing approach, you should calculate the time it will take to action each item. Then lay out the time line that you will work through to do the marketing. This will help you prioritize your activities, and get an idea of when you will have to spend money. Your marketing time line does not have to be too elaborate, but make sure the times are realistic. Table 2 is an example of a marketing time line. On the CD you will find a blank Marketing Time Line to help you complete your own time line.

TABLE 2
MARKETING TIME LINE

Activity	Elapsed Time	Completion Date	Comments
Develop a slogan	2 days	2 April	
Develop/make business cards	3 days	7 April	
Develop stationery	2 days	9 April	
Develop website content	6 days	17 April	
Have website designed	15 days	10 May	
Obtain website hosting	10 days	10 May	
Develop brochure	3 days	22 April	During website work
Print brochures	5 days	29 April	During website work
Develop marketing letter	3 days	28 April	During website work
Customize/address marketing letters	8 days	8 May	During website work
Mail marketing letters	1 days	9 May	During website work

6. The Marketing Plan

You can put all of the above activities together into a comprehensive marketing plan that you will refer to in the future, and no doubt modify as you gain more experience in acquiring business. Or, you can just include the marketing elements in your overall business plan that is discussed in Chapter 12. Appendix A has a sample business plan that includes the marketing plan.

MARKETING MATERIAL

1. Why You Need Marketing Material

You have to have marketing material to give to potential and ongoing clients. Business cards, brochures, and a good website are important marketing tools that you will need for your business.

You should also have more specific marketing material, such as a marketing letter if you are going to do direct-mail marketing. Tied in with the marketing letter, you may want to have a response form that the potential client can easily use to contact you for more information. This chapter will help you develop these marketing tools.

2. Business Cards

Business cards are essential because they enable people to contact you in the future. They can also remind a client about your business as he or she is sorting through his or her card files looking for something else.

You probably already know that you can design and print your own business cards very easily with today's word processing programs, and blank business cards are available at most stationery stores. The following are a few tips on business card design:

- Your business card should contain the name of your company and logo (if you have one), your name and position (e.g., president, manager), your business slogan, and your contact information (e.g., telephone, fax, email). You can add your business address as well, but if your business is in your home and you are worried that showing your home address will detract from your business image, you can rent a postal box and use that as your business address.

- Keep the card simple and uncluttered. People who read business cards normally spend only a few seconds looking at a card, and are primarily looking to see what your business does.

- Include your business slogan that describes what you do, with a catchy phrase if possible.

- Make sure your company name and logo stand out by using the largest print, then your name and business slogan in a quickly readable size print. Your contact particulars should be in smaller print.

3. Business Stationery

Stationery stores have a huge variety of business stationery stock on which you can print your message. You can also design a fancy letterhead for your letters and envelopes, and have a printing company make them for you — at considerable expense. However, the least expensive approach, and just as effective, is to use ordinary white paper with a letterhead that you can print each time with your own printer. The following are some tips on designing your letterhead:

- Your company name and logo should be in the largest print on the page, then your business slogan in a quickly readable size font. Your contact particulars should be in small print. All of this should not take up too much of the page because you want to have plenty of room for your letter.

- Design your letterhead in black and white so it can be easily printed with a standard laser printer. Color increases your printing costs considerably. Many large companies have gone to black and white letterheads to save costs.

4. Website

A good website not only tells people what you do, but also enables them to start communicating with you. Your website is a marketing tool that you can use to get the interest of potential clients. If you can get your website situated high on search engines, it can be a very powerful business magnet.

You can design and set up your own website, but unless you are very experienced at this, it is probably better if you hire a professional web designer to create it. Even if you have your site professionally developed, you will still have to supply input about the design. This input will most certainly be the informational content, and you will probably want to be involved with the overall design as well. You therefore have to have a bit of knowledge about websites. Of course you can Google keywords such as "website design" and find many sites that will provide you with information. The following sections provide some basic information about websites.

4.1 Domain name

The domain name is the address of your site, such as www.mybusiness.com. Every domain name ends in a top-level domain name, which is always either one of a small list of generic names, or a two-character territory code. The generic names are usually of three characters following a dot (e.g., .com, .org). The two-character territory code is also following the dot (e.g., .ca for Canada).

There is an international system of organizations and commercial companies that control the domain names. You will have to register your domain name with a domain name registrar that is accredited by the Internet Corporation for Assigned Names and Numbers (ICANN).

There is an annual charge for the domain name registration. A few companies have offered low-cost or free domain registrations. However, this deal usually comes with a requirement that the company hosts your website for a price, and/or you tolerate their third-party advertisements on your website.

4.2 Web host

You have to have a web host for your website. This is the company that has your website on its computer. Web hosting is a big business and there are thousands of companies offering this service. Most of these companies also offer help in designing your site.

To find a web host simply Google "web host," and you will be inundated with web hosts. A good comparison of website hosts, for both American and Canadian host companies, is at www.Web-Hosting-Reviews.ca. Your best solution is to choose a company that caters to small companies like yours, by helping you develop your site, hosting it, and also handing feedback to you.

4.3 Website design

Whether you design your website yourself, or have a professional do it, you will have to make some decisions regarding the site, and provide other input. First of all, you should consider your design criteria. The following are some things to consider.

⊟ Purpose: Is the site to be just informative, or do you want it to generate business for you and act as a feedback method for potential clients?

⊟ Audience: Who are you aiming the website at? Will it be sophisticated Internet users or casual Internet users? Will the audience want fancy graphics or basic text information? Will they want to quickly contact you through the website?

You must include the following items on your website:

⊟ Your business name and slogan.

⊟ A description of what you do for clients.

⊟ Your contact information.

You might also consider some of the following items on your website:

⊟ A Client Request for Proposal form that he or she can complete quickly and automatically email to you requesting information and quotes for your services. See Appendix E for a sample of this form. There is also a blank form included on the CD for your use.

⊟ If a potential client would like some general information about your company, then you may want to add to your website a general form such as an Information Request. An example is included in Appendix E and a blank form is included on the CD.

- ⊟ Examples of your work (with the previous clients' permission).
- ⊟ List of clients (with their permission).

4.4 Content

The content of your website will be arranged in a series of pages, beginning with a home page that the reader sees first. Make sure that the information on the home page is clear, precise, and sufficient to grab the reader's interest enough for him or her to look further. The home page must convince the reader that your business can help him or her.

The home page must convince the reader that your business can help him or her.

The remaining information pages must also be clear and precise. The information pages should not contain anything that does not support the purpose of the website, or is not of interest to the target audience. Also, be very careful with gimmicky artwork that could distract the reader from your message.

4.5 Keywords

Keywords are the secret to getting listed on Internet search engines. Typically, search engines look for keywords in your page titles and in your page contents. The number of times a keyword appears is the keyword density, which is used to rate your site in the search engine output. There is considerable information available on the Internet about keywords, and you should look into this marketing tool to bring potential clients to your website.

4.6 Search engine listing

You can also go through a process to have your website listed with the search engines. The following are the websites that explain the process for the top three search engines.

- ⊟ Google: www.google.com/addurl/
- ⊟ Yahoo: www.search.yahoo.com/info/submit.html
- ⊟ MSN: search.msn.com.sg/docs/submit.aspx

5. Brochures

Brochures tell people what you do. A brochure can be given to potential clients, used in direct-mail advertising, and used in many other situations.

The content of your brochure can be taken from your website, and vice versa. It does not have to be a graphic artist's masterpiece, but can be on ordinary paper that you print yourself. It is the content that matters, and here are some suggestions:

- Focus the content to match your target audience.

- Catch the reader's attention by emphasizing you will help him or her in his or her business. Make this the opening statement of the brochure and use a larger font to capture the reader's attention.

- Explain briefly how you will help the potential client.

- You may want to give a description of what you will deliver to the client.

- Briefly describe your company.

- If possible, give a few testimonials or list some impressive clients. It is important that you ask your clients for permission to use their testimonials before you use them in your brochure.

- Provide contact information (e.g., email address, telephone number, fax number).

- Keep the brochure simple, with short, hard-hitting text. Make sure your brochure does not appear too cluttered.

- Highlight important aspects with larger font size, but do not have too many different fonts and font sizes.

6. Marketing Letters

If you are going to do a direct-mail advertising campaign, via either postal mail or email, you will have to have a marketing letter. There are two approaches you can take with the marketing letter. You can put your whole marketing message in an all-inclusive letter, or you can have the letter just introduce an attached brochure.

6.1 Brochure introductory letters

The letter introducing a brochure is usually used in postal mail to personalize the contact with the recipient's name and address (see Sample 2 at the end of this chapter). It can also be used in email, but the brochure should be a continuation of the main body of the email and not an attachment (see Sample 3 for an example of an email letter). Here are some tips on drafting brochure introductory letters:

⊟ In postal mail use the standard business type letter, with the recipient's name, position, and address at the top left, followed by "Dear Mr. Whatever." For email begin with "Dear Mr. Whatever."

⊟ The opening sentence should grab the reader's attention immediately by telling him or her how you are going to help him or her. Keep the opening sentence as brief and as hard hitting as possible. Remember that the recipient of the letter may only spend a few minutes, or maybe just seconds, on the initial look at your letter. So you have to grab the person's attention quickly. Then elaborate a bit, but not in great detail. Your brochure will give readers more details about the services you offer.

⊟ In the second paragraph give a brief description of what you will deliver to the client. This paragraph should also direct your reader to your brochure for additional information. You should also direct the reader to your website.

⊟ In the second or third paragraph provide a brief description of your service, and how to contact you. Again, you can refer the readers to the brochure for more details.

⊟ Finally, quickly thank the person for his or her time, and provide your name and company position (e.g., president, marketing manager). In emails also add the company name under your name. In postal mail the company name will be on the letterhead, but you should actually sign the letter above your printed name.

6.2 All-inclusive marketing letters

The all-inclusive marketing letter, without a brochure, is a much bigger challenge. You must get your whole marketing message in a brief, hard-hitting letter, preferably on a single page. There is not much space to do this, after you allow for the letterhead, the recipient's address, the salutation, and your signature block. But it can be done. The tips to writing the all-inclusive letter are similar to those of the brochure introductory letter discussed in section **6.1**, but you have to add more detail about what you will do for the client, your service, and how he or she can contact you.

For examples of all-inclusive marketing letters, see Sample 4 and Sample 5 at the end of this chapter.

7. Client Response Form

You should have a client response procedure built into your website, and you should also have an old-fashioned hard copy response for direct-postal mail. The main purpose of a client response form is to make it easier for the potential client to contact you. You want the client to be able to quickly complete the form and have it sent to you right after he or she reads your letter and brochure. It is almost like an impulsive purchase.

The following includes some tips on drafting your client response form:

- Your form should be faxable, with your fax number on it.
- Keep the form simple so the client can quickly complete it, preferably by simply checking boxes.
- Ask for enough information from the potential client to enable you to qualify him or her as a serious prospect.
- In some lines of business, you may also want the client to provide enough information for you to send him or her a proposal.

Sample 6 at the end of this chapter is a sample client response form.

8. Unsolicited Email

You should be aware of laws governing the sending of unsolicited email. The following information is not legal interpretation or advice, but only information obtained from the Internet.

In the US, the CAN-SPAM Act of 2003 (*Controlling the Assault of Non-Solicited Pornography and Marketing Act*) establishes requirements for people who send commercial email. The law is explained any the Federal Trade Commission website at www.ftc.gov/bcp/conline/pubs-/buspubs/canspam.shtm. Please visit the website for more details.

The law states the following:

- You cannot use false or misleading header information. This means that your email address and name must identify you as the person who sent the email.
- You cannot use deceptive subject lines. Your email subject line cannot mislead your intended recipients.

- Your email must give recipients an opt-out method. Your email must include a return email address or link for the person to send you a request not to send further emails to his or her email address. If a person does ask that you no longer send emails to him or her, you must honor the person's request.

- Your commercial email must be identified as an advertisement and include your valid physical postal address.

In Canada the *Personal Information Protection and Electronic Documents Act* (PIPEDA) touches on email issues. However, Canadian government legislation is current being considered regarding unsolicited email. See www.privcom.gc.ca/keyIssues/ki-qc/mc-ki-pipeda_e.asp for more information.

BROCHURE INTRODUCTORY POSTAL LETTER

Construction Technology Update   *Helping You Compete*
123 Any Street, Anywhere, NY 12345
Tel: 555-123-4567 Fax: 555-123-4560

January 5, 2009

Clive C. Goode, Engineering Manager
Megaproject Construction Company
Somewhere, MI 67890

Dear Mr. Goode:

Technology changes in the construction industry are rampant, and Construction Technology
Update can help you keep up-to-date with these changes.

We can provide technology searches for specific construction challenges, and/or we can keep
you informed of new developments with a monthly report. We cover all areas of the construction
industry, including new developments in techniques, materials, equipment, tooling, and building
codes. You specify the coverage you want. The attached brochure will explain our services in
detail, or you can visit us at www.ctu.com.

Construction Technology Update has been serving the construction industry since 1992, and has
developed a huge database to monitor the industrial changes.

Thank you for your consideration.

Yours truly,

I. M. Asearcher
President

SAMPLE 3
BROCHURE INTRODUCTORY EMAIL LETTER

Dear Mr. Goode:

Technology changes in the construction industry are rampant, and Construction Technology Update can help you keep up-to-date with these changes.

We can provide technology searches for specific construction challenges, and/or we can keep you informed of new developments with a monthly report. We cover all areas of the construction industry, including new developments in techniques, materials, equipment, tooling, and building codes. You specify the coverage you want. The attached brochure will explain our services in detail, or you can visit us at www.ctu.com.

Construction Technology Update has been serving the construction industry since 1992, and has developed a huge database to monitor the industrial changes.

Thank you for your consideration.

I. M. Asearcher, President
Construction Technology Update

POSTAL LETTER WITHOUT BROCHURE

Construction Technology Update
123 Any Street, Anywhere, NY 12345
Tel: 555-123-4567 Fax: 555-123-4560

Helping You Compete

January 5, 2009

Clive C. Goode, Engineering Manager
Megaproject Construction Company
Somewhere, MI 67890

Dear Mr. Goode:

Technology changes in the construction industry are rampant, and Construction Technology Update can help you keep up-to-date with these changes.

We can provide technology searches for specific construction challenges, and/or we can keep you informed of new developments with a monthly report. We cover all areas of the construction industry, including new developments in techniques, materials, equipment, tooling, and building codes. You specify the coverage you want, and our reports will be directed to your company with your needs in mind. The technology developments we report are detailed, with evaluations if available, and information on how you can access the technology.

Construction Technology Update has been serving the construction industry since 1992, and has developed a huge database to monitor the industry's changes. Our clients range from small, specialized construction companies to large, international firms. To quote one of our clients, "CTU keeps us up-to-date on what is happening in our industry allowing us to take advantage of changes."

You can visit us at www.ctu.com for additional information, or contact me at 555-123-4567, or email me at asearcher@ctu.com. You can also complete the attached Client Response Form and fax it back to us. Based on the information you provide, we can send you a proposal and price for our services.

Thank you for your consideration.

Yours truly,

I. M. Asearcher
President

EMAIL LETTER WITHOUT BROCHURE

Dear Mr. Goode:

Technology changes in the construction industry are rampant, and Construction Technology Update can help you keep up-to-date with these changes.

We can provide technology searches for specific construction challenges, and/or we can keep you informed of new developments with a monthly report. We cover all areas of the construction industry, including new developments in techniques, materials, equipment, tooling, and building codes. You specify the coverage you want, and our reports will be directed to your company with your needs in mind. The technology developments we report are detailed, with evaluations if available, and information on how you can access the technology.

Construction Technology Update has been serving the construction industry since 1992, and has developed a huge database to monitor the industry's changes. Our clients range from small, specialized construction companies to large, international firms. To quote one of our clients, "CTU keeps us up-to-date on what is happening in our industry allowing us to take advantage of changes."

You can visit us at www.ctu.com for additional information, or contact me at 555-123-4567, or email me at asearcher@ctu.com. You can also complete the attached Client Response Form and fax it back to us. Based on the information you provide, we can send you a proposal and price for our services.

Thank you for your consideration.

I. M. Asearcher, President
Construction Technology Update

CLIENT RESPONSE FORM

To: *Construction Technology Update, 123 Any Street, Anywhere, NY 12345*

Fax: _555-123-4560_   Telephone: _555-123-4567_

Please send us a proposal to provide a monthly report on *[add information]* changes in the following areas. (Please check areas you are interested in.)

- ☐ Techniques
- ☐ Materials
- ☐ Equipment
- ☐ Tooling
- ☐ Building codes

I am specifically interested in the following aspects of the industry. (Complete only if desired.)

Please send the proposal to:

Name: _____ Position: _____

Company: _____

Postal Address: _____

_____

_____

Email Address: _____

Telephone: _____ Fax: _____

Website: _____

Please fax this to: *Construction Technology Update, at fax number: 555-123-4560*

8

GETTING THE CONTRACT

This chapter discusses contracts, but the information herein is not to be considered legal advice. The information provided is presented for basic informational purposes only, and legal advice should be obtained from a qualified legal source.

1. Types of Contracts

A contract is when one party makes an offer and another party accepts it. The written contract is evidence of this agreement. The written contract can vary from a simple letter agreement or purchase order, to a very complicated document involving thousands of pages. For your Internet research business you will only have to have very basic contracts, such as the following types of contracts.

1.1 Contract for a specific project

The contract for a specific project is a very simple contract for a specific research project, such as finding the latest methods being used to solve a particular construction problem. A special task contract is included as Appendix F at the end of the book.

1.2 General service contract

The general service contract is an agreement that you will work for a client for a specific time period and the client will pay you on a defined hourly or daily rate. This is a very good arrangement for you.

1.3 Retainer contract

The retainer contract is similar to the general service contract. You agree to do work for a client for a specific time period and the client will pay you on a defined hourly or daily rate. However, the client agrees to pay you a minimum for each month or other period of the contract, even if he or she does not use your services. This is an even better arrangement for you. An example of a retainer contract is included as Appendix G at the back of the book.

2. Contents of Contracts

There are many terms and conditions that can be included in business contracts. Not all of them are required for your contracts, unless of course your client insists on them. Here are the suggested basic provisions you should have in contracts with your clients:

- Identification of the parties: The name and address of both you and your client.

- Purpose of the contract: For example, "To provide Internet research services."

- Areas to be researched: As agreed to by you and your client.

- Duties of each party: What you will provide to the client, such as a final report, and what the client will provide to you, such as information on his or her product.

- Delivery dates: This is the date that you will deliver the information to the client. This may not be required in some contracts, such as an annual service contract.

- Client company tasking authorities: This is applicable in annual service contracts, and defines the client company official or officials who are authorized to task you under the contract.

- Method of tasking: This is applicable in annual service contracts, and defines how the company will task you. For example, tasking may be by postal letter, email, or telephone, from the authorized company official.

- Payment terms: The agreed price for a project, or hourly rates for a service contract.

- Nondisclosure agreement: You agree not to disclose any privileged or confidential client information to anyone else.

- Signatures of authorized signatories: Your signature, and the signature of the client's person who is authorized to make the agreement or the purchase.

3. Contract Agreements

Contract agreements do not have to be too elaborate in your Internet research business. You just want to make sure you and your client understand what you are to do, and that you will get paid for doing the work. The following sections are the types of contract agreements you will probably work under.

3.1 Verbal tasking

Verbal tasking may occur when you are under a general service contract or retainer contract. The client may email or phone you and ask you to do a specific task, under the existing contract. This method of tasking should be specified in the contract document.

3.2 Letter contract

The letter contract is a very simple way to contract for a specific task. The letter can be originated by you and written to the client, or originated by the client and written to you. For example, if you initiate the contract letter, in the letter you stipulate the task, the delivery date, and the price. In the last paragraph of the letter, you ask the client that if he or she agrees with the terms in the letter, he or she sign it and return it to you. You sign the letter with your signature block. At the bottom of the last page of the letter put the statement, "I agree with the terms in this letter," and have an area for the client to sign with his or her signature block, the company name, and the date. Appendix B contains a sample letter contract.

3.3 Purchase order

The purchase order is usually used to purchase goods, but it can also be used to purchase services. You may want to help the client in drafting the purchase order, as discussed in section **4.2**. Once you receive the client's purchase order, on his or her standard format, you are in business.

If you can help your clients with the contracting process, the better it will be for everyone.

3.4 Detailed contract

The detailed contract is a more involved contracting procedure. You or the client draft a detailed contract document including all the provisions listed in section **2**. These provisions are negotiated and amended as required, then you both sign the contract document. Appendix C contains a sample general service contract.

4. Help the Client Close the Deal

Clients are busy people. If you can help your clients with the contracting process, the better it will be for everyone. The following sections are some tips to help you close the deal with your client.

4.1 Send the client the letter contract

By sending your client a letter contract as described in the section **3.2** and in Appendix B, you make life easy for him or her. All the client has to do is sign the letter and return it to you.

4.2 Help the client draft the purchase order

You are helping the client if you suggest wording for him or her to put in the purchase order and you are also helping yourself by ensuring the work is properly defined. If you have made a proposal to the client, you can suggest that his or her purchase order say, "For services as detailed in the ABC Internet Research Inc. proposal dated … " If it is for a specific task, you should also suggest a delivery date and price that would be put into the purchase order.

4.3 Help the client draft a detailed contract

You help the client by drafting the contract, which the client can amend if he or she wants to. You then send the client two copies of the agreed contract, both signed by you. The client signs the copies, keeps one copy for his or her records, and returns the other signed contract to you. Appendix C has a sample general service contract.

5. Written Proposal

There will be many situations in which you will have to offer prospective clients a detailed, written proposal. There are many books and articles on how to write proposals, but these are usually for larger projects. Appendix D contains a sample proposal.

Each proposal is different, but the main items you should cover are as follows:

- Understanding the requirement: Your understanding of what the client wants you to do. You will base the rest of the proposal on this understanding.

- Objectives: What you will accomplish for the client. Try to be as specific as possible. You might even mention future projects that could emerge from this project, but that are not part of this proposal.

- Statement of Work (SOW): This is a common part of larger proposals and contracts, but it also applies in smaller form to your work. This is where you explain to the client how you will do the proposed work. However, you do not want to be too detailed, because if you are to detailed, the client may get somebody else to do the work with your guidance in your SOW.

- Deliverables: What you will provide to the client, such as a final report.

- Follow-on work: If applicable, you can mention some of the follow-on work that could evolve from this contract, but do not make it sound like a lot of work or you may scare the client away. If you do not anticipate any follow-on work from this contract, leave this section out of the proposal.

- Price and schedule: How much you will charge the client, and when you will deliver the reports. For larger, longer projects you may want to consider progress payments linked to defined milestones in the project, such as the completion of Phase 1, the preliminary investigation.

- Confidentiality: You should assure the client that you will not give away any of his or her business secrets.

- Your qualifications to do the work: A brief description of your company, your experience, and possibly your previous clients (with their permission). This is your commercial to convince the prospective client that you are the one to do the work.

6. Interfacing with Clients

There are four main times when you will have to interface with clients:

- To get the contract.

- To do the work.
- To explain any problems the client has with your deliverables.
- To get a follow-on contract.

This interface will probably be a mixture of emails and verbal conversation, either face-to-face or on the telephone.

Your first interface with the potential client is as a salesman to get the contract. If you can, find out why and when the client wants the work done, and make your sales pitch accordingly. You can find out what the client's thoughts are by asking questions such as, "What do you want this project to accomplish?" You can also make comments such as, "You and your staff can probably do the work, but do you really have the time to do it?" Then you have to close the deal. If the prospect is still skeptical, ask why he or she is skeptical, and then reassure him or her. You can close the deal by saying things like, "Can I email you some information to put into the purchase order?"

You next have to interface with the client when you are doing the work, but keep it to a bare minimum. The client is a busy person; remember, the person hired you to save him or her time. So don't bother the client unless you absolutely have to.

You will have clients who complain about your work and your deliverables. Don't take it too personally. Some people are just born complainers. Try to accommodate these clients as best you can, but if there is no hope for follow-on work, do not waste too much time on them.

Finally, you should interface with the client for follow-on work. You can even start this while you are working on the project by dropping hints that some other aspects relating to the work should also be considered later on. Then, after you deliver the final report, you can contact the client to see if he or she has any questions about it, and at this time offer to send the client a proposal to do the follow-on work.

Even if there is no possible follow-on work associated with the current project, you must keep in contact with the client on a regular basis in order to get other work from him or her. Repeat business can be very good for you, but you have to work at it. The client will forget you if you do not keep in touch on a regular basis. Do not overdo it. Contacting the client monthly or every second month is good. The following are some suggestions for how you can keep the communication open:

- Send the client an email about a website you ran across that pertains to his or her business.

- Send the client some additional and/or recent information that applies to the project you did for him or her.

- Ask the client if there are any other projects you can do for him or her.

- Send the client a Seasons Greetings card.

- Ask the client to go for lunch.

PROJECT ESTIMATING

1. Work Breakdown Structure

The work breakdown structure (WBS) is the basic tool for project management and estimating. It breaks down any size project into progressively smaller work packages, in a tree-like structure. This enables each work package to be properly scheduled and managed, but equally important, it allows the project to be estimated from the ground up. In each small work package, time and costs are estimated, and all of these costs are "rolled up" to obtain the overall project cost.

Even though your Internet research projects may not be very large, you should still develop a WBS for each of them. It will enable you to do a fairly accurate estimate of how much time you need to do the job, and that translates into the price you should quote for it. When you get the contract, the WBS will help you properly manage your work on it. The following example explains the WBS process.

Example

Construction Technology Update (CTU) is a company specializing in keeping the construction industry up-to-date on the latest construction techniques, materials, equipment, tooling, and building codes. CTU was asked by a client to find out the latest techniques in relocating very old, stone, heritage buildings. In order to give the client an estimate of the cost of the job, CTU had to do a WBS of the project.

The CTU staff first broke the project down into the following major work packages:

- ⊟ Learn about the building to be moved.
- ⊟ Study recent examples of similar projects.
- ⊟ Study new techniques under development.
- ⊟ Make recommendations based on the findings.
- ⊟ Draft and submit a report.

They then had to break down the major work packages into smaller packages that could be estimated:

- ⊟ Learn about the building to be moved.
  - ⊟ Visit the building.
  - ⊟ Visit the new site.
  - ⊟ Talk to appropriate people about the building.
  - ⊟ Document the issues about moving the building.
- ⊟ Study recent examples of similar projects.
  - ⊟ Develop keywords for an Internet search.
  - ⊟ Find recent examples of similar projects.
  - ⊟ Extract relevant information from similar projects.
  - ⊟ Document the relevant information.
- ⊟ Study new techniques under development.
  - ⊟ Find new techniques under development.
  - ⊟ Assess the new techniques.
  - ⊟ Document the relevant information.
- ⊟ Make recommendations based on the findings.
  - ⊟ List relevant information in order of applicability.
  - ⊟ Make recommendations.
- ⊟ Draft and submit a report.

- ⊟ Structure the report.
- ⊟ Draft the report.
- ⊟ Produce the report.
- ⊟ Deliver the report.

2. Time Estimating

Once you have a work breakdown structure, you can then make your time estimates. For the Internet research business it is appropriate to estimate by the hour. For each item in the WBS, estimate how much time you think it will take you to do. Give this serious thought, because a lot depends on your estimates. If the estimates are too high, the client may reject the project. If the estimates are too low, you will lose time and money on the job. You will probably never get an estimate exactly right, even after considerable experience in doing it. However, as you gain experience you will get closer to the correct numbers. The following example illustrates the estimating process associated with the WBS process developed in the previous example.

You will probably never get an estimate exactly right, even after considerable experience in doing it. However, as you gain experience you will get closer to the correct numbers.

> *Example*
>
> *The first work package to be estimated was "Visit the building." The staff estimated it would take about an hour to drive to the building location, and an hour to return. The worker would have to spend about two hours looking at the building, taking notes, and talking to whoever was available. Thus the total for the first work package would be four hours.*
>
> *Each of the smaller work packages was similarly considered and estimated. These numbers were then rolled up for each major work package. The resulting numbers were as shown here:*
>
> ⊟ *11 hrs — Learn about the building to be moved*
> - *4 hrs — Visit the building*
> - *2 hrs — Visit the new site*
> - *3 hrs — Talk to appropriate people about the building*
> - *2 hrs — Document the issues about moving the building*
>
> ⊟ *9.5 hrs — Study recent examples of similar projects*
> - *0.5hr — Develop keywords for an Internet search*
> - *3 hrs — Find recent examples of similar projects*

- *4 hrs — Extract relevant information from similar projects*
- *2 hrs — Document the relevant information*

⬦ *8 hrs — Study new techniques under development*
- *3 hrs — Find new techniques under development*
- *3 hrs — Assess the new techniques*
- *2 hrs — Document the relevant information*

⬦ *3 hrs — Make recommendations based on the findings*
- *1 hr — List relevant information in order of applicability*
- *2 hrs — Make recommendations*

⬦ *9.5 hrs — Draft and submit a report*
- *0.5 hr — Structure the report*
- *4 hrs — Draft the report*
- *3 hrs — Produce the report*
- *2 hrs — Deliver the report*

Now it was possible to estimate the time it would take to do the complete project, by simply adding the time estimates for all of the major work packages. In this example the total time to do the job was 41 hours.

After you have completed your time estimates, you should go back and review them to make sure you got them right. This is especially required if you think the estimates are too high or too low. You will be surprised at some of the changes you make in your estimates when you look at them a second time.

Example

The CTU staff was concerned with the high total time estimate for the job. They went back and had a second look at each work package estimate. They were able to reduce the item "Visit the building" from four to three hours, and the item "Talk to appropriate people about the building" from three to two hours. Thus the first major work package, "Learn about the building to be moved" was reduced by two hours to nine hours. The other work packages were similarly reviewed. Some were increased in estimated time and others were reduced. The net result of the review was to reduce the overall project time estimate to 34 hours.

3. Labor Costs

Once you have the time estimates totaled, it is a simple matter of multiplying the estimate by your hourly rate to get the labor cost for the project.

Example

The total time estimate of the project in the above example was 34 hours. At a charge-out rate of $85 per hour, this made the labor cost $2,890.

4. Additional Costs

You next have to estimate any additional costs you may encounter with the project. Standard office costs such as computer time and stationery are already covered in the overhead charges you incorporated in your charge-out rate. However, you have to charge extra for items such as project related travel.

Example

In the previous example there were two trips that had to be accounted for. The first one, to the building site, was estimated as 25 miles away, for a two-way total of 50 miles. The trip to the new site was 35 miles, for a two-way total of 70 miles. Thus the total travel cost associated with the project was estimated to be 120 miles. At an allowance of $0.32 per mile, the travel cost was estimated to total $38.40.

In certain states and provinces you may also have to charge taxes. For example, in Canada all goods and services sold have to add on the Goods and Services Tax or GST. You do not have to show these taxes on your proposal to your client, but you will have to include them in your final billing to the client as separate items.

5. Contingency Allowance

You should also allow for some contingency in your quote to the client. This gives you some protection in case you erred in your time estimates, or other cost estimates. A standard contingency is 10 percent or 15 percent of the estimates. So after you have your labor costs and other costs totaled, you then add the contingency percentage for the final quote.

Using the numbers from the previous examples in which the labor cost estimate was $2,890, and the travel cost was $38.40, the total estimate was $2,928.40. Adding a contingency of 10 percent, or $292.84, brings the total to be quoted to $3,221.24.

6. Buy-in Considerations

Sometimes it is appropriate to quote a reduced estimate price to a new client just to get that all-important first job. In other words, you buy in to the work. This slight reduction often pays dividends in future work from the client. The reduction to be considered should make the quoted number look attractive. For example, a buy-in price of $2,995 is much more appealing than $3,221.24.

7. Price and Delivery Quotes

With your time, labor costs, additional costs, and contingency worked out for the project, you are then ready to make your price and delivery quotation to the client. The price quote will be the number you worked out after you added in your contingency. However, for optics you may want to round off the number, or buy into the job because of future work possibilities.

Example

The total price of $3,221.24 in the previous example was rounded off to $3,200. However, it was decided that since this was a new client, it would be more impressive to keep the price less than $3,000. The final quote to the client was $2,995.

For your delivery quote go back to your WBS time estimates. If this is your only job to be done over the anticipated time frame, you may be able to devote eight hours a day to it. However, remember that you can only average about three days a week, or about 24 hours a week, to billable work. (See Chapter 5, section **4.**, for a discussion on billable time.)

If you will be working only on this project, divide the WBS total time estimate by 24 to get how many weeks it will take you to do the work. To be on the safe side, add in an extra week or two.

Example

The total estimated time of the example was 34 hours. Dividing this by 24 indicates that the work should be done in approximately 1.4 weeks. Rounding this off to two weeks, and adding two weeks for unforeseen events, makes the time about a month. The quoted delivery date is one month after receipt of order.

TIME MANAGEMENT

1. Why You Must Manage Your Time

Many people think that when you own your own business you don't have to work as much, and you can take time off whenever you want. In fact, if you are going to make the business successful, the opposite is true. You will probably work more hours than if you were employed by somebody else. You will also find that you are working at odd times such as weekends and evenings, just to meet deadlines. Sure, you can arrange to take time off whenever you want, but it usually has to be done around business commitments. This is why it is so important to be able to effectively manage your time.

People also think that those who work at home don't really work as diligently as they would in an office environment. This can be true. There are many distractions at home that can rob you of your work concentration. Children are an obvious distraction. Then there is the closeness of the kitchen, with its available snacks that can beckon you. The games on your computer can also be enticing, since there is nobody to see you playing them. All in all, working at home can be a challenge, and you have to be very disciplined in your work habits and time management.

2. Establish Your Work Area and Work Routine

When you work for somebody else it is usually in an office or other specific work setting, with others around you. There is usually an established routine of when the workday starts and ends, the lunch breaks, etc. It is pretty easy to follow the work routine along with everyone else. But if you work at home, a structured routine is not available unless you create it. In addition, you have the distractions mentioned in the previous section. So it is vitally important to establish a working regime if you are going to effectively manage your time.

The first step in establishing an effective working regime is to set up a proper workstation. Ideally, you want to have a dedicated office for your work. Typically, this is a spare bedroom in the house, or an area in the basement. The items you will need in your home office are similar to most business offices, but you will have to provide them for yourself. The following is a list of the main items you will need, in rough order of priority, with those you can get later at the bottom of the list:

- ❏ Desk: This is the most obvious item because it is like the driver's seat in a car. This is where your business happens. The desk is not only what you work on, but it also contains most of your working tools, active files, coffee cup, etc.

- ❏ Computer: This is another obvious item, particularly for an Internet research business. It can be a desktop or a laptop model. Each have their advantages and disadvantages. The desktop model comes with a relatively larger standard keyboard, and it enables you to have a larger and wider screen. Computing power and data storage used to be greater in a desktop, but laptops are now available with similar capabilities. The advantage of a laptop is that you can take it with you for client presentations, and research at other locations. If you want a bigger screen and keyboard, many laptops have connections that will allow you to use them. You will also need an Internet connection.

- ❏ Computer work programs: Various business packages are available, but the best one is Microsoft Office. This is not an ad for the product, but it is recommended because it is the most widely used. You risk the possibility of annoying a client if you deliver a report to him or her in a word processing program he or she doesn't have. Almost everyone has MS Word. Also, do not get suckered into buying special programs that do fancy report publishing or desktop publishing. MS Word will do these functions quite well, and your client will be able to open the file you send him or her.

- Printer: You are better off with a good black and white laser printer. They are cheaper to operate, and usually much faster than color printers. If you occasionally need a color printer, get an inexpensive one in addition to the laser printer.

- Telephone: Initially you may want to use your home phone, but you will soon find you need a dedicated business phone line coming into your house. This is especially true if you live in an area in which you have to use a dial-up connection to the Internet.

- Fax: You will eventually need a fax machine to receive client purchase orders, tasking, and for many other reasons. Many telephone companies offer a business phone that can have two separate telephone numbers on one line, with one number having a single ring and the second number having a double ring. You can then have your fax connected to the second number.

- File cabinets: You will need to keep hard copy files, so you should have a file cabinet in which to arrange and store your files.

- Shredder: A shredder helps keep your work, and your client's business, confidential.

- Accounting software: A simple accounting software program will save you a lot of office work, and they are relatively inexpensive. Ask your accountant what program he or she would like you to use.

You also want to establish a working routine that you can stick to, and avoid time-killing disruptions. First establish how many hours you want to work each week, and which days you want to work. If you want to work the business full time, 40 hours a week, you will probably set yourself up to work 8 hours each working day of the week. If you want to be semi-retired, and only work part time, you will have to decide how many hours you want to work each week and when. For example, you could work a few full days and take the rest of the week off, or you could work a few hours each day. Some people work in the mornings, and spend that earned income in the afternoons on golf courses or other hobbies.

The concept of project management is to carefully plan and organize the project into smaller defined activities, arrange the activities in a logical sequence, then work on the activities in that sequence.

After you have decided on how many hours you will work a week, set the time of the day you will start and the time you will quit. Let your family know your routine so they can avoid interrupting you during your working hours. Your clients will also get to know when they can contact you in your office. Most importantly, a fixed routine will help you manage your time, and greatly increase your productivity.

3. Project Management

Project management is an essential part of time management. The concept of project management is to carefully plan and organize the project into smaller defined activities, arrange the activities in a logical sequence, then work on the activities in that sequence. This prevents you from duplication of some activities, and working on activities that depend on other activities you have not yet completed. You can do very simple project management by hand, or you can use a sophisticated computer program to do it.

The key to good project management is to develop a good work breakdown structure (WBS), which is explained in Chapter 9, section 1. For most projects you will encounter, you will have a pretty simple WBS, and so you will be able to do a very simple but still effective time management of the project. Just write down the logical and required sequence of the activities, and assign the estimated time to do them. Then work out your estimated completion times and dates for each activity. As you then work through the project you can keep track of whether you are on time with your work, ahead, or falling behind.

There are numerous project management computer programs available. Most are far too powerful and complicated for your requirements, but a relatively simple one can help you manage each of your projects and save you time. Once you have entered your activities into the program, and indicated those that depend on the completion of others, the program will work out the sequence of activities for you. When you also attach the estimated time to be spent on each activity, the program will automatically work out the start and end dates of each activity. As you work on the project, and inform the program that you have completed activities, it will let you know if you are on schedule or not. It will also tell you when you should complete the overall project.

4. Gathering and Storing Information

As you work on a project it is easy to collect a huge amount of information and spend a lot of time revisiting it as you write your report. An easy way to keep control of the information is to create a separate file folder on your computer for each contracted project. You can then put all project related files into the computer folder, and you may even have to break it down into sub-folders. Include in these folders copied website pages on which you found relevant information. When you are writing the report, and you need some additional information on a particular aspect that you already covered from a website, you can easily go back to the site to see if there is more information for you.

If you have a number of projects from a particular client, you should put them all together in a client company named folder. As future projects come in from that client you can easily scan your files to see if there is any old information that can be used on the new project. If you have a lot of projects from one client, you can periodically transfer the information onto a CD as a backup copy.

You may also want to set up a three-ring binder to collect and sort information on a project. Use dividers for each activity identified in the WBS, and as you work on the activities put the information into the appropriate place in the binder. Include printed copies of informative websites you run across, and using a highlighter pen, highlight the parts that are relevant to your project. Highlighting the appropriate information when you first read it will save you a lot of time later when you are writing the report, and you only have to read the highlighted parts of the printed information. Also, the printed page should have the website address on it, which will enable you to return to that website for more information if needed.

Saving information you gather in a way that will allow you to efficiently retrieve it is a major time saver. It may appear to take more time when you are doing it, but the payoff will come when you are writing the report for the client. Another payoff may come on a future project when you require similar information.

5. Multitasking

In any successful business you will find yourself juggling several client projects or your own company activities. This multitasking can cause you to waste time, as you go back and forth from one activity to another, and have to get back up to speed on what you did the last time you were working on the project. There are simple ways to manage this problem and your time.

When you have to stop working on a project for a while, take the time to jot down on a Post-it Note what your next steps are in the activity, and any other things you should remember about it. Put the Post-it Note on the project binder, or in a safe place on your desk. When you return to the project you will know immediately where to resume work and you will not have to waste time going over what you previously did, which makes it easy for you to determine what to do next.

6. Recording Websites

As you work through a project you will run across many websites. Some will be more useful than others, and some will be useless. Since the useful ones probably pertain to your specialty, you should keep a record of them so you can use them in future projects. You can use the Internet sites listed in the Resources file on the CD as a start for your website recording. You will probably have to expand the subject listing to encompass your own specialty requirements. You will find that the list of sites grows quickly, so once again, try to make it as retrievable as possible to help you manage your time.

CHAPTER
11

DOING THE WORK

1. Verify the Client's Needs

Once you have confirmed your contract with a client, the first step in doing the work is to make sure you fully understand your client's needs. This should have been resolved with your proposal, and the subsequent contract negotiations, but in the haste to secure the contract something may have been overlooked. Also, there may have been some semantic problems during the negotiations, in which you and the client had different understandings of some words or phrases.

A good way to verify that you understand the client's needs is to study the client's website, brochures, and general way of doing business. You will have to do this anyway when you write the report because it should include how the information you found impacts on the client's specific business. If you do it now, the activity will guide you in your investigative work and ensure a suitable result. Also, you may realize some subtle changes are required to effectively do the contracted work the client wants.

Example

An information researcher was contracted by a small North American cosmetics manufacturer to identify suitable business partners to work with in Asia. When the researcher took a closer look at the client's website, he discovered that the client was already associated with a company in Russia. The researcher telephoned the client to find out about their Russian partner, and it turned out to be a business horror story. The Russian company had taken the delivered cosmetics, changed the labels to their own, and sold them as their own. Then the Russians had stopped purchasing some of the cosmetics, and the North American cosmetics manufacturer suspected that they had copied the product and were now manufacturing it themselves.

After a bit of discussion the researcher realized that the client did not want to find partners in Asia, but wanted to find suitable distributors or agents for the products. This would make quite a difference in the type of Asian companies to look for. Partners could be companies that made their own cosmetics, as well as resold products made by others. Distributors bought large quantities of the product and resold it to retailers. Agents simply arranged for retailers to purchase the products from the North American manufacturer.

The phone call with the client helped the researcher verify that the work was really to find suitable distributors or agents and not a partner.

2. Beginning the Information Search

The actual information search starts with establishing keywords to use to begin an Internet search. Do not limit the keywords to what it says in your contract, but think outside the box to see if there are any other words or phrases that could apply. As you work with the words you begin with, you will probably run across other areas of the information that you or your client never thought of. Follow up these other areas as well. This is the sign of a good Internet researcher, someone who digs up valuable and relevant information that the client never considered.

However, a word of caution about going off in other directions. Though it is sometimes fruitful to go in other directions, it can also be a waste of time, particularly if you find some interesting but irrelevant sites to explore. You will need to discipline yourself and get back to your list of search words and phrases when you find yourself too far off the path.

Sometimes, following up in other areas can save you a lot of work. You may find that some website already has a large portion of the information you are seeking. You will of course have to verify and validate the information, and in so doing you may find other valuable information.

The search engine business is very competitive because of the advertising revenue search engines can earn.

> *Example*
>
> *The information researcher in the previous example began his work by searching with keywords "agent + Asia + cosmetics" and "distributor + Asia + cosmetics." The initial search came up with 175,000 results, far too many to check out individually. However, one of the top ones was BUYUSA.GOV, a site of the US Commercial service, and it described an upcoming trade show COSMOPROOF Asia, The Asian Beauty Event. The site also listed 14 Asian agent/distributor companies who were looking for products to work with. Now it was a matter of checking each listed company.*

3. Internet Search Engines

You have probably already used some of the many search engines that are available on the Internet, such as Google and Yahoo!, but there are many more. Some are highly specialized, concentrating on a specific area of information, and others are very limited in what they cover. The Resources section on the CD provides a listing of Internet search engines, as well as other Internet sites that you may want to investigate.

According to Nielsen NetRatings, the market share of search engines in August 2007 was as shown in Table 3.

TABLE 3
MARKET SHARE OF SEARCH ENGINES, 2007

Company	Market Share %
Google	53.6
Yahoo!	19.9
Microsoft	12.9
Time Warner (AOL)	5.6
Ask.com	1.7
Others	6.2

*statistics from Nielsen NetRatings August 2007

There are even search engine reference sites such as the Search Engine Guide that lists and links you to specialized search engines. The Search Engine Guide has a searchable directory of general and specialty search engines. The site also includes resources and tools to help you explore deep into the web and perform advanced research.

The search engine business is very competitive because of the advertising revenue search engines can earn. To keep competitive the search engine providers are constantly upgrading their service to get more searchers and hence more advertisers. The service these search engines provide is of course to your advantage, if you can put up with the accompanying advertising.

You should also remember that there is a thriving industry of companies that, for a price, help other companies get their websites onto the search engines. They not only ensure that their client sites come up on the search engine results, but they strive to get them as close to the top of the results list as possible. So the first few results of a search engine search may not be the best. Keep working down the list to ensure you get as much information as possible.

4. Free Internet Information Sites

There are now many Internet sites that gather information on particular subjects and make it available on their sites. A popular subject is financial information on companies, and this is often required information if you are assessing the viability of a company. However, many of these sites are limited in the companies they cover, and the information they provide. The information can also be dated. Nevertheless, it may be all you need for a particular project.

Local governments and chambers of commerce often have listings of businesses in their community, and the information is sometimes quite detailed. They usually also provide considerable other information about their community. All of this is very useful if you are researching locations for a client, trying to get information on a company, or trying to find companies.

5. Charging Internet Information Sites

There are also many Internet sites that charge for information. They lure you in with a small amount of the information you are seeking, but when you ask for more they direct you to a page on their website that asks you to sign on as a member — for a price. Others will give you free membership, but when you want a particular report they charge you for it.

Nevertheless, some of the information sites that charge are very reputable and have been around in other business formats for decades. One such site is that of D&B, who provide financial and credit information on companies around the world. Their main website is at www.dnb.com, and they have websites for specific countries, such as www.dnb.ca for Canada. They usually charge by the report you request.

There are also many organizations and learned associations who charge for their reports and papers. One such website is that of the Institute of Electrical and Electronics Engineers (IEEE), one of the world's leading professional associations for the advancement of technology.

The cost of obtaining reports from a website that charges varies from around $10 or less a report to several hundred dollars per report. For example, InsideDefense.com gives you the first three reports you request for free, but after that the site charges $10 per report. D & B has a graduated scale; they charge around $60 for basic financial information on a company, and about $150 for a very detailed report. Sometimes it may be cost-effective for you to pay to become a member of one of the charging information websites, or pay for a particular report or paper. However, make sure that the information the site provides is what you want, and in the detail that you need.

How do you get compensated for the money you spend on obtaining a report for a client? It is probably better if you absorb the cost and not get the client involved. If you try to charge the client for it, he or she may think, "Why didn't I just get the report myself and save the money I'm paying this person?" Also, the time and cost of the paperwork to charge the report to the client may be much more than the report cost. So just absorb the cost. After all, it probably saved you a lot of time, which could mean money in your pocket.

6. Misinformation, Disinformation, and Half-Truths

The information available on the Internet should always be verified, by checking it with several sources. If it is misinformation, it could be because of errors on the part of the person who posted the information. For example, the popular Wikipedia site is a free encyclopedia that includes valuable information but it can also have errors in it. Most of the published information on Wikipedia is written by volunteers who do not get paid for their work. So the old adage can apply: You get what you pay for.

The more dangerous situation is that of disinformation, that is, posted information purposely designed to mislead the readers. Probably the worst of this disinformation is the hate literature that is posted on a site intended to spread the warped views of some organization or person. Then there are the hackers who get into a site and make unauthorized changes, usually on political sites. Of course, you can easily run across a site that just has plain lies, which is intended to mislead the readers. With a little common sense you should be able to identify disinformation, usually by a quick investigation of the source.

Half-truths are more difficult to identify and are usually not posted with any malicious intent. It is usually a situation in which the information has been paraphrased or only some of it is posted to comply with the aim and/or guidelines of the website. Like all the information you gather on the Internet, verify it by checking it at other information sources. The following example illustrates how half-truth information can hurt you if you don't check it out.

> *Example*
>
> *The information researcher in the previous examples came across an Asian website that listed a number of agents and distributors of cosmetic products in various countries. For each of the companies listed, the researcher took the time to go the company website to see who their customers were, who their suppliers were, the size of the operations, and the locations. Several companies appeared to be ideal distributors for his client. One in particular stood out because it claimed to have offices in several countries. A company like this would be perfect for the client.*
>
> *As part of the verification process, the researcher also did a search using each company name. He was astonished to see a magazine article on a new factory the company was setting up in Malaysia that would manufacture cosmetics and export them around the region. The company was indeed a distributor, but mainly of its own products that they may be copying from others. This was exactly what the client was trying to avoid. Had the researcher just used the initial half-truth information it could have developed into a very difficult situation.*

7. Other Information Sources

As you become more proficient in your searches, you will discover information sources other that the Internet. Books, magazines, and newspapers can provide a lot of background information for projects you may be contracted to work on. The books of course are available in the public library, as are many of the magazines and newspapers. They are also available in bookstores at a cost, but don't hesitate to buy what you need if the price is right. For example, if a $40 book is going to save you several hours of work, it may be cost-effective for you to make the purchase. You may also be able to use that reference in future projects. However, be careful of copyright issues.

Governments provide an astonishingly amount of information, and some of it is quite useful. More and more of that information is available on the Internet, but there is also the old-fashioned way of getting information by communicating with people. You will have to have patience trying to speak to the right person, because governments are notorious for passing you on to other departments. However, when you do find someone who knows what he or she is talking about, it may have been worth the agony. People are often quite eager to pass on their knowledge, particularly if you can add to it by giving them some information.

Information on your country's embassies around the world is usually available on the web. The trade officials are often all listed according to the areas of commerce for which they are responsible. In the following example you will see how the information researcher utilized the embassies for his research.

Example

The information researcher in the previous examples listed the possible distributors he had identified according to the country in which they were located. He then found the name of the appropriate trade official at the embassy of each listed country, as well as the official's email address and/or fax number.

He sent emails or faxes to the trade officials asking them for whatever information they could provide on the distributors listed in their country. Some officials did not respond, but most of them did, usually with a list of agents and distributors of their own. This provided some validity to the information the researcher already had.

8. Drafting the Report

The report you send to your client should not only provide the basic information you found for him or her, but you should also analyze it as much as you can, and recommend what the client should do to use the information.

Begin your report with a short synopsis of your findings. This is sometimes called the Executive Summary. The purpose is to give the reader a short burst of the most important information in the report. If the client wants more, he or she will have to read the whole report. Although the Executive Summary goes at the beginning of your report, it is written after you have written the main part so that you can summarize what is in the report.

You should start the main part of the report by stating the type of information that you searched for, based on the agreement you made with the client. This should deflect any arguments from the client if he or she thinks you missed looking into a particular aspect. By stating what you covered, you will also leave the door open for more work if the client wants to broaden the search.

Do not bother to detail your methodology, unless some of it is relevant. For example, if you checked out a large number of sources but only a few were significant, you may want to mention the numbers just to show how much work you did. But do not get too detailed — the clients want results not an academic thesis.

Present your findings in a format that the client can use immediately, without having to do any further interpretation, and try to show how it will impact on his or her business. For example, if the client has asked you to identify companies he or she should approach for business, you should do a preliminary assessment of the ones you identify. Estimate the chances of the client doing successful business with each company, and perhaps give the businesses a rating of high, medium, and low. Then organize them in the priority you think the client should approach the companies.

End your report with conclusions and recommendations. The conclusions will be your interpretations of the information. The recommendations are your suggestions on what the client should do with the information you provided. For example, you may want to present the client with a list of recommended action items. You can divide the list into immediate action items and long-term action items. If you think there is more work to be done, say so. Remember not to use too much detail — save that for a future proposal that you may suggest the client ask you for.

Appendix H includes a sample report.

THE BUSINESS PLAN

1. Why You Need a Business Plan

Developing and writing a business plan will force you to think about your business in detail. It will make you think seriously about issues such as the market, and how much money you will make. It will also make you think of issues that you would probably not consider otherwise. Some of these issues may be good, some bad, and one or two may even be total showstoppers that indicate a nonviable business. In general, as you develop your business plan you will get a much more detailed idea of your future.

Business plans are often used for the company to get loans or sell shares. You may want to use it to get a bank loan or a personal loan from a friend or relative. However, in all likelihood, in your one-person business, the main person reading the business plan is you. You have to believe and stand by the statements you make. So be honest and make sure you don't paint an overly rosy picture of the future business. By the same token, don't reduce the expectations if you think they can't be as high as they seem.

There are many sites on the Internet that tell you how to create a business plan. Also, there are numerous books on the market that cover the subject in minute detail. Your business plan does not have to be too elaborate, but it should include the following subjects covered in the next sections. Many of these have already been covered in previous chapters. The business plan puts the following together in a single document:

- Business opportunity
- Deliverables
- Company structure
- Potential clients
- Competition
- Market share of clients
- Marketing procedure
- Sales procedure
- Project work procedure
- Working team
- Projected revenue
- Projected expenses
- Profit/loss analysis
- Financing
- Future expansion
- Action time line

The following sections describe what should go into each of the above sections of the business plan. Appendix A has a sample business plan that you may want to read in conjunction with the text in this chapter.

2. Business Opportunity

You will already have considered the business opportunity when you developed your business model in Chapter 3. For this part of the business plan you can use the information in the business model. That is, what you understand to be the client's potential problem, how you can solve the problem for the client, and what value or benefit your activity is to the client. However, for the business plan you may want to add some additional information about your background and qualifications for doing the work. This information may also be useful in your marketing efforts.

Example

Mr. C spent many years marketing for various military manufacturing companies. He got to know the military acquisition process, the way military industrial companies did business with the military, and the R&D process of both. Late in life Mr. C was laid off without much hope of getting another job. He recalled that one of the marketing efforts he usually found successful was going through the military budgets to see if there was any business opportunity for the company he worked for. This was usually a very successful way to get new business leads, and he wondered why more companies didn't do it. He decided to start his own company that would search for client business opportunities in the US military, by going through the published US military budgets.

Appendix A contains a sample business plan of Mr. C's military budget business opportunity service. His first part of the business plan was to describe the business opportunity and the benefits that would be provided to the clients.

3. Deliverables

In your business plan you should detail what you plan to deliver to the client. This will help you in developing your project work procedure, and in doing your estimates. You will also be able to use this information in your marketing and sales efforts.

Example

Mr. C considered what he would like to see from an Internet researcher if he was a client. He would want the report in clear, concise terms, listing the opportunities in order of win probability. He would not want just a list of the opportunities, but he would also want a brief description relevant to his business. Most importantly, he would want information on who to contact to start the pursuit and the contact details of that person. Finally, it would be nice to see a suggested pursuit plan. Mr. C put all of this in his business plan that is shown in Appendix A.

4. Company Structure

Having read Chapter 4, you will probably have decided on the type of company structure you will have. Your next step is to choose a name for your business. Your business name is very important if you decide to create an incorporated company because your name cannot be similar to that of an existing company. As part of the incorporation process, you will have to pay a service that verifies which similar names are already being used by other companies. If your chosen business name is too close to an existing one, the incorporation authorities will not let you incorporate. You then have to choose a different name.

For a sole proprietorship the rules are more relaxed. This is particularly true if you use your own name in the name of the company. If possible, you may want your company name to describe what you do. However, do not make the name so long that it is cumbersome.

Example

Mr. C decided to start small with a sole proprietorship. If the business grew sufficiently, it could be incorporated later. In considering a name for the company, he initially thought of Military Budget Opportunity Service, but that seemed a bit long and awkward. He finally settled on Military Business Opportunities (MBO). The name not only is a partial description of the business, but it also hints that many opportunities are available.

5. Potential Clients

You will have identified your potential market numbers in the business model you developed in Chapter 3. For the business plan you may want to elaborate more and include the location of the potential clients and any other information that will help you in your marketing efforts.

Example

Mr. C knew most of the military industrial associations. He had been a member of many of the associations and he had attended many of their conferences. He decided that the best list of potential clients for his business would be on the website of the Defense Industries of America (DIA). He went to the website and discovered that the site listed approximately

1,400 members. These were companies seriously involved in the defense business. The listings, in alphabetical order, also provided a direct link to each company's website. He would use this in his marketing efforts later on.

6. Competition

You have to consider the competition in your business plan, because it will affect your market share. In most service businesses there are two types of competition — direct and indirect.

Your direct competition consists of the companies that offer the same service that your company offers. These can usually be identified by web searches, or in a very localized area by the telephone *Yellow Pages*.

The indirect competition is a little more difficult to determine. It depends a lot on the type of business you offer and is usually associated with the potential clients themselves. The most common indirect competition is the attitude of your potential customer — the client thinks he or she can do the work himself or herself even though this person doesn't have the time to do it. The potential client can in effect be your competition. You cannot really quantify this competition. All you can do is estimate a percentage of the potential market that will be affected by it.

Example

Mr. C did an Internet search for military budget search services using several combinations of the term. Although each search resulted in a number of hits, when he checked them he realized that most were not involved with what he was planning to do. A few Washington lobbying companies offered what sounded like a search of military budgets for client business, and Mr. C assumed that these would probably work with the large military companies. Nevertheless, he listed them as competition.

A form of Mr. C's indirect competition would be the fact that some companies were component suppliers to other military manufacturing companies, and would not be interested in the budget search service. As he scanned the list of companies, Mr. C realized that approximately 30 percent of the companies were only component suppliers and probably not interested in his service.

In your first year of business you will only be able to market cost-effectively to a small number of potential clients.

Mr. C also realized that he would meet resistance from potential clients who would want to do the budget searches themselves, even though they probably did not have the time to do so. He assumed that this would be a major portion of the available companies, perhaps about 60 percent.

7. Market Share of Clients

Once you have identified the number of potential clients, you can get an estimate of your possible market share of clients by subtracting the numbers taken away by the competition, both direct and indirect. Remember, these are only estimates, and the real numbers will evolve as your business proceeds. In your first year of business you will only be able to market cost-effectively to a small number of potential clients. Thus you will only have a small number of contracted clients. The numbers will increase as your marketing becomes more effective, and some of your clients stay with you from year to year. Your market share of clients must be considered to build over a few years' time span.

Example

The number of potential clients estimated for the MBO service was 1,400. Of these approximately 15 percent were large companies who probably had other arrangements to search military budgets, and would not be interested in MBO. This reduced the 1,400 down to 1,190. Similarly, approximately 30 percent of the 1,400 listed companies were small component suppliers probably not interested in MBO, reducing the number by 420 to 770. Finally, of this remaining number about 60 percent will want to do the work themselves and not be interested in contracting MBO. Thus the estimated market share of clients would be approximately 308.

Mr. C was impressed by this number of probable clients. However, he realized that the business would be slow to develop and the total number of clients would be spread across several years. He assumed that the 308 clients would have to be obtained over a five-year build up, and the annual numbers can only be estimated. He assumed that only about half of the contracted clients would stay with him from year-to-year, with the other half opting for only a one-year contract. He estimated the number of clients he could expect to have each year as follows:

Year 1	*24 clients*
Year 2	*36 clients*
Year 3	*50 clients*
Year 4	*80 clients*
Year 5	*118 clients*

8. Marketing Procedure

The marketing procedure you intend to use in your business should be explained in your business plan, and the cost of it should be estimated. The reason is that this could be a major expense, which must be considered in the business plan. Also, as you think about it, write it down, and put a price on it, you will probably develop a more cost-effective procedure.

Chapter 6 discusses marketing and the development of a marketing plan, of which an abridged version should go into your business plan. Chapter 7 covers marketing material, including website issues. Your costs for marketing must be in your business plan.

An example of marketing procedure is included in Appendix A, section **7**. The projected costs associated with the marketing are included in Appendix A, section **12**.

9. Sales Procedure

The sales procedure is how you will close the deal and secure the contract with a client. The costs associated with the sales procedure are usually not high, but the costs and the procedure should be included in your business plan.

Chapter 8 discusses how you can conduct the sales procedure to get the contract. Appendix A, section **8**., provides an example of this portion of the business plan.

10. Project Work Procedure

Your business plan should address the project work procedure because this will affect your revenue and expenses. Chapter 11 discusses how you go about doing the work of an Internet researcher. This part of the business plan describes that work procedure as concisely as possible.

You will probably amend the procedure as you gain more experience, but by documenting it in the business plan you have a starting point. Also, later on as your business grows and you have to hire or contract for help, the documented procedure will be a part of training your new assistants.

Once you have laid out the procedure, you can then estimate the time it will take you to do each part of a typical contracted Internet research job. Visualize the project and estimate how many hours each part of the procedure will take. The total will give you an estimate of how much time you will take on each contracted job. This number is needed in your revenue and expenses calculations, and you may also be able to use it in your marketing and sales efforts.

See Appendix A, section **9.**, for an example of the project work procedure in a business plan.

11. Working Team

In all likelihood, your initial work team will be you alone. In this section of your business plan you will have to calculate the hours you can devote to doing the contracted work, as well as doing the company marketing, sales, and administration tasks.

Chapter 5, section **4.**, discusses the issues of billable time, company time, and personal time. In Appendix A, section **10.**, it gives an example of working time calculated in a business plan.

12. Projected Revenue

The maximum revenue you yourself can earn in a year is simply the amount of billable time you have available in a year, multiplied by your charge-out rate. However, this assumes you will have sufficient contracted work to fill all of the available time. You may reach this point in your second year of operation, but during your first year you will take a while to bring in clients.

You can also calculate how many contracts you will have to win to fill all that billable time. Based on your calculations on how much time it will take to do an average contracted project, and how many hours you have available for billable time during a year, you can calculate how many projects you can do a year.

Example

Mr. C calculated his maximum revenue per year and arrived at a figure of $105,840. He also calculated his estimated revenue over the first five years, based on his market share calculations. These numbers are all shown in the business plan in Appendix A, section 11.

13. Projected Expenses

The projected expenses will be those similar to most companies. The financial outlay for your small company can be grouped into the following categories.

13.1 Personnel

Initially your personnel costs will be your own salary. Unless you have other income sources, you need a salary to live on. You have to make arrangements to make this monthly payment to yourself no matter what the company cash flow situation is.

13.2 Website

You will probably have to pay to have your website designed and uploaded. You may also want to pay some company to maximize the search engine hits on your site. Hosting the website will cost you a monthly or annual fee.

13.3 Marketing and sales costs

Marketing and sales costs will be a continuous expense because you will always have to work at bringing in business. There are several ways to estimate these expenses, but for the purposes of your business plan you may want to calculate these expenses on a per client basis. The methodology of doing this is explained in the sample business plan in Appendix A, section 12.

13.4 Delivery cost

The delivery cost is not a large expense, but sometimes it can be expensive if the client insists on you giving him or her a verbal report along with the written report. Also remember that the delivery of the written report will incur postal mail or courier expenses.

13.5 Office overhead costs

Office costs will mainly be the cost of your Internet connection, computer equipment, amortization, telephone, and standard office supplies. These costs are discussed in Chapter 5, section **2.**, as well as in Chapter 13, section **6.**, in relation to income tax.

14. Profit/loss analysis

After you have calculated your estimated revenue and expenses, you can create a profit/loss analysis. The profit/loss analysis is projected for a period of time, such as five years. For an example of a completed profit/loss analysis see Appendix A, section **13**.

The best way to create a profit/loss analysis is to use a computer spreadsheet program. There is a blank Profit Loss Calculations form in MS Excel included on the CD for your use.

You begin your profit/loss calculations by entering your estimated projected revenue in each of the five years. This will be based on the number of contracted projects you anticipate. You can list the number of contracted projects across the top of the spreadsheet. Since the revenue and often a portion of the expenses are tied to the number of contracted projects, it will help the spreadsheet do the calculations if these numbers are shown. Your revenue is the number of contracted projects multiplied by an estimated average price of the projects.

Expenses should be broken down into relevant categories. In the MBO example in Appendix A, expense categories are personnel, contracted help, website, marketing and sales, delivery, and overall office costs. The highest expenses for your company will probably be the personnel costs, that is, what you pay yourself. However, make sure you account for all of your other estimated expenses as well.

The bottom line of the profit/loss analysis is just that: your profit or loss. You get this by simply subtracting your expenses from your revenue. In all likelihood, it will show a negative number in the first year. This is a loss that most companies incur when they start up. However, there should then be a slow build of business over the subsequent years. In the MBO example the fifth year shows a profit of $70,512. This, in addition to the personal salary of $60,000, projects a total income for the owner of $130,512.

15. Financing

You should have some form of financial plan that will enable you to cover your expenses if you do not have the revenue to do so. This is usually a requirement for the first year, or sometimes the first few years. The financial plan often involves a loan or bank line of credit.

The bank line of credit is an arrangement with the bank whereby you can draw money out as you need it, and repay it when you can. You only pay interest on the money you owe at any time. The bank of course will put a limit on the amount of your line of credit. (Lines of credit can be taken out by companies or individuals.) Since your company will probably not have a sufficient track record to satisfy the bank, the bank may want you to take out a personal line of credit based on your equity such as your home. Although, if your Internet research business and your business plan looks good to the bank, it may give your company a small line of credit at a fairly high interest rate.

16. Future Expansion

Most companies want to expand because more business means more profit. You will probably want to expand as well, and this should be reflected in your business plan. Expansion is based on more business, which translates into more revenue. However, this also brings on more expenses, particularly the cost of hiring more people to complete the work.

There are two ways for you to hire additional help — by taking others on as employees or by taking others on as subcontractors. If you take on regular employees, you will have to pay them a regular wage. You must make sure you have enough additional business to keep them busy earning revenue for you so you can cover the wages. Otherwise, you may have to let them go. Also, in some states and provinces you may have to pay for health plans and employee insurance. Of course you will also have to do the paperwork associated with their income tax. You may want to think hard about hiring staff.

The alternative is to hire people to work as independent contractors, where you pay them for each job they do for you. This eliminates most of the problems discussed in the previous paragraph. Most importantly, you only pay the contractors for work you give them. If you do not have sufficient work for them, you do not have to pay them. Another advantage of contracting the work is that if the contractors are not able to do good work for you, you don't have to give them any more work.

A disadvantage is that as subcontractors gain experience in the business, they might go to a competitor of yours with your company secrets. Or worse, they might want to start a company in competition with your company. To protect yourself, you should get them to sign a nondisclosure agreement that legally prevents them from telling others about your company. Also, you should get them to sign a non-compete agreement to stop them from setting up a business similar to yours.

Expanding from a one-person operation is difficult, but it can be rewarding if you can bring in enough work to keep others and yourself busy. In the age-old capitalist tradition, you can profit from their work. As shown in Appendix A, the MBO service could have a very good profit as the business expands.

17. Action Time Line

The action time line is a schedule for you to get your business going. By creating a time line you will see what you have to do and when you will have to do it. You can also arrange the activities in a logical sequence, thus avoiding some timing problems. If you diligently follow your planned time line, you can avoid procrastinating over which activity to do next.

You start your action time line by going through your business plan and listing all the things that you have to do. Then you arrange them in a logical sequence, such as having brochure development take place before you do a marketing mail-out. Also, you can do other activities while you are waiting for one to be completed. An example of this is that while you are having your website designed you can be working on other activities.

Once you have listed and arranged your activities, you have to estimate how long it will take to complete them. Not just the time you will spend on the activities, but also how long you have to wait for others to do something, such as printing brochures. In your time estimates write down the elapsed time, in either days or weeks. With the time estimates it is a simple matter to set up a time line or schedule. You can set it up on a project management computer program if you want to, but it is probably just as easy to list the activities and the date you want to do them, as is shown in the Appendix A, section **16**. There is a blank Action Time Line form on the CD ready for your use.

ADMINISTRATION

1. The Need for Administration

If you have a one-person company, you have to do everything yourself. This includes all of the administration or office work. You will find that there is a lot to do in this area, particularly around income tax time, and it has to be done no matter how long you procrastinate about it.

The secret to keeping up with the administrative work is just that: keep up with it. You will recall that Chapter 5, section **4.**, discussed billable time, company time, and personal time. It was suggested that you will probably have to devote half a day a week to company administrative time. It may be a good idea to actually schedule this time each week. You will find that you need the time to do the following things:

- Preparing invoices
- Chasing delinquent accounts
- Paying bills
- Banking

Client billable time is your bread and butter. You should have an accurate account of how much time you spend on each client project.

- Buying office supplies
- Keeping records
- Filing
- Bookkeeping
- Perparing and submitting income tax
- Perparing and submitting other tax
- Taking care of many other unforeseen office requirements

2. Keeping Time Records

You should keep track of all of the time you spend working for your company. That is, your time spent on marketing and sales, administration, and of course, on client billable time.

You will no doubt spend much more time on marketing and sales during your first year as you get your business started. You will have to continue to do this activity even after your business is well established. You want to keep a record of the time you spend on a project to make sure your pricing reflects the actual costs associated with getting clients.

Similarly, your administration time will be high during the first year as you set up the business. You will have to continue to do this after your business has been established and keeping track of your administration time will help you in your pricing as well. Accurate records of how you spend your administration time will allow you to look into time savings, such as hiring part-time hired help to take over some of this burden.

Client billable time is your bread and butter. You should have an accurate account of how much time you spend on each client project. This is particularly important if you are working on a project where you charge for the time you spend on it. Projects that you contracted for at a specific price also have to be accounted for, for two main reasons:

- To see if you made a profit or a loss on the project.
- To verify your time estimate and make improvements in your estimating process.

You do not have to keep track of time to the nearest minute. Keeping track to the nearest six minutes, or one tenth of an hour is fine. This also makes the totaling easier since you are dealing with hours and decimal point portions of them. The simplest way to keep track is to write down on a slip of paper the date and the actual time of day that you start working on something, with a word or two explaining what work was done. When you are finished working on that activity, write down the time you finished then total the time you spent on it. Record this amount of time on a daily/monthly record that can be recorded on either a hard copy, such as a day planner, or on a computer spreadsheet.

Sample 7 is a daily/monthly time record sheet. On the CD you will find a blank time sheet in both MS Word and MS Excel that you can set up as a spreadsheet on your computer. In a spreadsheet program you can have it automatically total up the monthly hours you spend, as well as other information such as total monthly time. The sample has columns for company administration, marketing and sales, and three different client projects you are working on. If you have more projects during the month, simply add more columns.

3. Billing the Clients

You will probably bill your clients at the end of a project, when the deliverable to the client includes:

- ⊟ The project report.

- ⊟ The billing invoice in a standard form.

- ⊟ A covering letter that talks about the report, the invoice, and makes recommendations for further work, if applicable.

- ⊟ A fax form for future information searches.

The billing invoice will have your company letterhead on it, and particulars of the client project. Sample 8 is an example of a standard invoice. On the CD you will find a blank invoice that you can use.

The items that should be on your invoice include the following:

- ⊟ Your company letterhead.

- ⊟ Your slogan (if you have one).

- ⊟ The name of the client company.

- ⊟ An invoice number used for your own tracking purposes. The client's payment to you will probably reference your invoice number.

TIME SHEET

CTU Time Sheet — June 2009

Date	Day	Company Admin	Marketing & Sales	Megaproject Construction	Fabulous Cosmetics	Teach Yourself
1	S					
2	M		6.6			
3	T		4.3			
4	W			2.5		
5	T			6.7		
6	F	3.4		7.4		
7	S			2.6		4.6
8	S					
9	M	2.5				3.6
10	T					3.6
11	W					7.0
12	T		7.4			7.3
13	F					6.4
14	S					
15	S			5.6		
16	M	1.5				6.5
17	T			6.6		
18	W			6.8		
19	T			2.6		
20	F	2.5	5.3			
21	S					
22	S					
23	M		6.4			
24	T	3.8			2.7	
25	W				6.2	
26	T				2.5	
27	F				4.8	
28	S					
29	S					
30	M		6.2			
TOTALS		**13.7**	**36.2**	**40.8**	**16.2**	**39.0**

Monthly Total   **145.9**
Approximate Weekly Average   36.58

- The billing date.

- The client's contracting reference, which is usually his or her purchase order number or date.

- The name of the project.

- The billed-for activity date, activity description, hours charged, and the charge, which is the number of hours multiplied by your charge-out rate.

- Remember to add the taxes if required in your state or province. In Canada, all goods and services are subject to the Goods and Services Tax, so this must be added to the charge for time, and the total must be billed to the client.

You can also add late payment charge information at the bottom of the invoice, such as, "Accounts in arrears by more that 30 days will be charged an additional 2% for each month or portion thereof in arrears."

4. Collecting Payments

Most clients will eventually pay you, but sometimes it may take a while. Their accounts payable people may wait the standard 30 days before they issue payment, and then it may take a few weeks before you receive the payment. You may not see any money for about two months after you send them the invoice. This is not an unusual situation.

If you do not hear from a billed client in three months, you should do something about it. Your invoice may have been lost, some other administrative glitch may have taken place, or your client may just have forgotten to authorize the payment. Do not be reluctant to send a polite query letter or email to the client. You can hide it somewhat by asking if there are any questions regarding the report sent to him or her, and then slip in polite words about not receiving payment yet. For example:

We have not yet received payment of our invoice dated March 7, 2009, and in case you did not receive it I am enclosing a copy of that invoice for your action.

You may, in some situations, have a client who refuses to pay for whatever reason. If the client does not respond to your polite requests for payment, you can threaten him or her with a letter saying you are turning the delinquent bill over to a collection agency. If the client

Construction Technology Update
123 Any Street, Anywhere, NY 12345
Tel: 555-123-4567 Fax: 555-123-4560

Helping You Compete

INVOICE

Date: June 25, 2009

Client: Megaproject Construction

Invoice No. 0806

Client Contracting Number: PO# 74808 dated April 26, 2009

Re: Heritage House Moving Information

Date	Activity	Hours	Charge
June 25	Research information regarding moving a heritage house	25	$2,250.00
	Plus tax at 5% (tax number 12345 7500 RT)	Tax	111.50
	Total amount now due		**$2,362.50**

I.M. Asearcher
President

Accounts in arrears by more that 30 days will be charged an additional 2% for each month or portion thereof in arrears.

SELF-COUNSEL PRESS — START & RUN AN INTERNET RESEARCH BUSINESS 08 still does not respond, carry out your threat. There are many collection agencies around who will go after the client to get your money, for a percentage of the outstanding bill. However, sometimes it may not be worth the effort and any resulting bad relationship to go after the money. You then may just want to forget the bill, and that particular client as well.

Another approach to the payment problem is to structure your projects into two or more phases. You make an interim report to the client after phase one, with an invoice. When you receive payment for that invoice you continue working on phase two, or withhold the final report until you get the initial payment. For example, your first phase of the project may be to identify new technologies associated with the client's request. Your interim report can list these technologies, and say that you are evaluating them and details of their applicability will be reported at the end of phase two. Your interim report will include an invoice, and you can withhold the phase two report until you get the interim payment.

5. File System

You need to set up a file system for your business to keep a record of what you have done. This will allow you to save time in the future when you have to do a project that is somewhat similar to something that you have done before. It may be client related, like a new project that is similar to one you did before, or company related, like a required marketing letter similar to a previous one. Your file system will help you from "reinventing the wheel," and you will be surprised at how often you will refer to it in the future.

Your file system can be simple or elaborate. Just remember, you want to make it easy to find and retrieve information from it in the future. The best way to set up the system is by starting with broad categories and reducing within the categories as your needs arise. You can number these files in a logical sequence so you can easily find them in a filing cabinet or in your computer. A simple yet effective system is shown in the following example.

Example:

This is a simple file system that can be used for computer files or paper files in a filing cabinet.

1000	*Administration*	
1010	*Company Legal*	
1020	*Office Equipment*	
	1021	*Computer*
	1022	*Internet*
	1023	*Furniture*
	1024	*Supplier Arrangements*
1030	*Couriers*	
1040	*Insurance*	
2000	*Promotion*	
2010	*Marketing & Sales*	
	2011	*Potential Clients*
	2012	*Website*
	2013	*Marketing Material*
	2014	*Sales Material*
2020	*Advertising*	
3000	*Financial*	
3010	*Banking Arrangements*	
3020	*Taxes*	
	3021	*Federal Income Tax*
	3022	*Income Tax*
	3023	*Sales Tax*
3030	*Accountant*	
3040	*Financial Accounts*	
	3041	*Year 2008*
	3042	*Year 2009*
	3043	*Year 2010*
4000	*Research*	
4010	*Free Internet Sites*	
4020	*Charging Internet Sites*	

<pre>
4030   Non-Internet Research
5000   Clients
5010   Annual Contracts
        5011   Fabulous Cosmetics
        5012   Teach Yourself
5020   Projects
        5021   Megaproject Construction — House Moving
</pre>

Your file system can be on the computer or in paper files in a filing cabinet. Computer files are handy because you can simply add additional folders within folders. However, there are some things that you cannot easily put in computer files, such as company incorporation papers or client mailed purchase orders. You will have to have both types of file systems.

6. Keeping Cost Records

You have to keep track of all of your costs, even though you may think they are not applicable to your business. You or your accountant can sort that out later. Get a receipt for everything, and keep it. The simplest way is with an organized "shoebox." Get yourself a card index box, with dividing cards for each month of the year. As you get receipts, put them in the box by the appropriate month. Periodically you and/or your accountant will have to sort out the receipts and enter them into your accounting system. Remember that costs can be used as tax deductions for your business.

7. Business Accounting

You can do your business accounting yourself, or you can have an accountant do it. An accountant will charge you for doing it, but it may be cost-effective for you to hire a professional. The accountant will probably complete the work faster and more accurately than you. This will leave you with more time to devote to clients.

If you plan to do the accounting yourself, buy some software to do it. There are numerous small business accounting software packages available on the market at reasonable prices. However, you may want to ask your accountant or tax preparer what program he or she would like you to use.

8. Tax

8.1 Income Tax

You cannot get away from income tax (federal and also state or provincial taxes). Like the business accounting, you can prepare your income tax submissions yourself or have a professional do it. The professional will not only do it faster and more accurately, but he or she may find additional deductions that you missed. Of course, the benefit is that while the professional is working on your taxes you can be working with clients.

You have to report all of your income to the government for income tax purposes, and there is nothing you can do to improve your tax situation in this regard. However, you can do something to ensure all of your legal deductions have been applied. Income tax rules vary from jurisdiction to jurisdiction, and sometimes it is not clear if a particular item can be deducted or not. If there is doubt, try it and see if your accountant or the authorities will reject it or not. Chapter 5, section **2.**, contains a comprehensive list of overhead expenses that you should consider for income tax deductions.

8.2 Other taxes

You may also have to consider other taxes, such as state and provincial sales tax. These taxes will vary from jurisdiction to jurisdiction, but if they apply to you and your business, you will have to deal with them. Accountants and tax preparers are usually up-to-date on all applicable taxes, and this is another reason you should consider hiring a professional.

Every US state has different tax regulations. For more information about state taxes for your business talk to a professional such as an accountant, or contact the Internal Revenue Service (IRS) for more information.

In Canada there is the Goods and Services Tax (GST). The rules are that all enterprises with revenue of more than $30,000 per year must register for the GST and make periodic (i.e., monthly, quarterly, or yearly) reports and payments. If the revenue is less than $30,000, registration is voluntary. Registered companies must charge the 5 percent GST on all of their sales, be they either goods or services. They must then report all of the GST they collected and make appropriate payments to the government. However, they are also allowed to report all of the GST they paid on company purchases, and deduct this from the GST they collected and have to pay to the government.

For a small start-up company it is actually advantageous to register for the GST. The revenue in the first year will probably be quite low, and so the GST collected will be low. However, the payments made on items to get the business going will be quite high during this initial period, and these payments all have GST attached to them. So it is possible that the GST on expenses could be higher than the GST on the revenue. In this situation the government refunds the difference to the registered company.

For more information about Canadian business taxes talk to a professional such as an accountant or contact the Canada Revenue Agency (CRA) for more information.

CHAPTER 14

EXPANDING YOUR COMPANY

1. Why You Should Expand

In the capitalistic world, you expand a company to make more money. Expanding the company usually means you'll be increasing the number of employees. With more employees you can take on more work, and more work makes more profit for the company.

2. Problems Associated with Expansion

Unfortunately, expansion comes with a number of problems. Most of them are related to employees, but there are other issues as well that you will have to address. The following are some of the problems you will face as you expand:

- Selecting the right employees
- Paying the employees
- Providing office space for employees
- Providing work-related equipment for employees
- Meeting government-imposed employee benefits

A company usually goes through several phases of expansion, and it usually happens over many years.

- Completing employee associated government paperwork
- Selecting the right middle managers
- Bringing in enough work for the employees

The last bullet is probably the most significant problem you will face as you expand, but the others can also be burdensome. Nevertheless, expanding your company can be very rewarding no matter how large you grow.

3. Phases of Expansion

Expansion doesn't happen overnight. It is usually an evolutionary process brought on by increasing contracted work. A company usually goes through several phases of expansion, and it usually happens over many years. The process is seldom planned, but it has to be managed to be successful.

Your initial phase of expansion will be the hiring of your first employee. You will do considerable soul searching about whether or not you should do it, how to find the right person, what to offer him or her, and what work to assign. Once you have hired someone, you will probably find it wasn't that much of an issue, and subsequent hirings will be easier. You will soon become quite adept at it.

The intermediate expansion phase is when you have to introduce middle managers into your company. This means you have to organize the company into some form of structure based on responsibility. It also means that you have to delegate some of the responsibilities that you have had up until this point to your middle managers. For some company owners this is difficult to do, but you have to do it if you want to grow the company. You cannot make every decision and do everything yourself.

Major expansion is way down the road for you, but hopefully, it will happen. Major expansion happens when you set up branch offices, make formal business alliances with other companies, and maybe even acquire other companies. This is a long way off, but keep the dream alive.

The final phase of your business expansion is your retirement from the company. This will probably be very difficult for you to do, but you have to face it eventually. The last section in this chapter will explain some of the options you will have.

4. Subcontract Employees

You have a number of choices regarding your first employees. You can hire somebody full time, or part time, or on a contracted basis. Hiring an employee, either full time or part time, involves a number of issues and problems that you may not want to deal with at this stage, such as the issues listed in the section **2.** bullet list. The best thing for you to do is to hire subcontracted workers. You can have them work in their own home, and on their own equipment, and only on projects you have available for them to work on. If there is no work, you do not have to pay them. Also, if they turn out not to be a good worker for you, you simply stop giving them work. This arrangement may require you to pay a little more in subcontractor fees, but it is certainly worth it because of the reduced risk to you.

How do you select suitable people to contract? You will want people who are knowledgeable in the type of work you do, and of course are fairly computer literate. Consider where you came from. If there are people in your old company who you think are suitable, perhaps they are interested in subcontracting with you as a part-time second job. They may also be thinking of retirement or a job change, and a small contract with you would be a good transition for them. Give your contacts a call and see what they say. If they are not interested, they may spread the word about the opportunity to others who are interested.

If you cannot find somebody from your old working environment, spread the word as best you can. Tell relatives, friends, and acquaintances that you are looking for somebody, and have them spread the word as well. Since you are going to hire someone under a subcontract, and not as a direct employee, you can even take a chance with a relative. Remember one of the advantages of contracted help is that if the contractor doesn't work out, you simply stop giving him or her work.

The first question a potential subcontract worker will ask is, "How much is the pay?" You will have to calculate how much you will pay your subcontractor beforehand. The easy way to do it is to go back to the calculations you did to establish your company charge-out rate. Simply reduce your own rate by your overhead, and your fee or profit. The hourly rate you end up with should be the maximum you will pay the new subcontract workers. If you pay them more than this maximum, you will be losing money. However, you must start at a lower rate to give yourself some bargaining room.

Example

In the price calculating example in Chapter 5, Mr. A established his price as $75 per hour. This was based on his estimated total annual overhead of $9,872 and his expected annual company income of $79,872. The overhead was (100 x 9,872 / 79,872) 12.36 percent of his established price. He also added a profit or fee of 10 percent. The overhead and fee made up 22.36 percent of his $75 per hour rate, or $16.77. The maximum he could pay a subcontracted employee is (75 − 16.77) $58.23 per hour. He decided to give himself lots of negotiating room, because he anticipated a range of competency in the people he would be considering. He set his minimum contracted pay rate at $40 per hour. This gave him a range of $40 to $58 per hour that he could work with in his offers to potential subcontracted help.

To task your subcontracted worker, you do not just give him or her a job to do on his or her own time, and then have the person send you a bill. You outline the task to the subcontractor and ask him or her for an estimate of the time it will take him or her to complete the task. If the subcontractor's estimated time falls within the time estimates you gave your client, task the subcontractor to get on with the job on the condition that you will only pay him or her up to the maximum time he or she estimated. If the subcontractor's time estimate is more than what you think the job will take, you will have to negotiate with your subcontractor to get the time below what you committed to your client.

You will also want to make sure the subcontracted employees do not tell others your company secrets, or worse set up a company in competition with you based on what they learned from you. In order to prevent this from happening, put a nondisclosure clause in the subcontract, as well as a non-compete clause.

The subcontract document itself can be a simple letter contract signed by you and your subcontractor. Appendix I has a sample letter contract.

5. Office Facilities

At some stage in your company expansion you will have to move out of your home and into a standard office setting. There are several options to consider in this move, each one with a different price tag. The least expensive option is to move into a facility supplied by a company that caters to start-up companies like yours. These incubator companies usually have a fairly large building that is divided into many small office spaces. You rent the amount of space you want and, as you grow, you can rent additional office space within the incubator company's building. The incubator company usually offers common conference room facilities that you can book and use when you need to. They often also supply a security controlled entrance to the building.

The next facility arrangement you may want to consider is to share facilities with another company that has more office space than it needs. This arrangement is somewhat similar to the incubator company option. However, there is a risk to you if the company you are sharing space with needs more space as it grows. You could be asked to move.

If you decide to skip the previous two options and rent office space on your own, you will have to consider the class of space you want and where it is located. This will determine the monthly or annual rental rate. You will also have to consider what your options will be if you have to expand even more later on.

When you do your cost calculations for renting your own office space you will have to consider two additional costs. The first addition cost to consider is any physical changes you may have to do to the space itself, such as adding walls, additional computer wiring, or lighting. You should be able to keep these costs down to a minimum if you selected the space correctly. The second big additional cost will be the office furniture such as desks, chairs, and of course computers. These costs can add up very quickly.

Another aspect you should consider when selecting new office facilities is the convenience for your employees. A little thing like free or inexpensive parking is very important to them. If you live in a big city in which many people commute using public transit, then being on a suitable public transit route will be important to your employees as well. Nearby lunch facilities such as a cafeteria are also a consideration.

6. Hired Employees

As your company expansion proceeds, you will have to move away from the subcontracted employees and hire full-time employees. This is a critical point in the company expansion, because now you will have a monthly payroll to meet. Your new staff will have to be paid whether there is contracted work for them to do or not. You should carefully consider the need for each new staff position.

The following are some other issues you will have to address when hiring employees:

- ▣ Job descriptions: You will need some form of job description for each position, if only to advertise the job opening.

- ▣ Selection of people: Selecting the right people to interview based on their résumés can be a time-consuming activity, as is interviewing those you do select for the interviews. It has to be done with considerable diligence, because these new people are part of your company.

- ▣ Pay rates: This is always a difficult issue. Make sure the pay ranges are established before you start the interviewing process. You can get information on pay rates from friends in other companies, and suggested pay ranges published by organizations.

- ▣ Government imposed benefits: Federal, state, and provincial governments have laws and regulations that force you to provide certain benefits to employees that you pay for. Make sure you research these thoroughly to ensure you are operating within the law, and identify what it will cost you to do so.

- ▣ Company benefits: Company provided benefits to employees do not have to be available in the early stages of expansion, but will eventually be required. These include health plans, dental plans, pension, or investment options.

- ▣ Support equipment: As mentioned earlier, you will have to provide support equipment to your new staff. This includes desks, telephones, computers, and general office supplies.

7. Company Organization

Early into your company expansion you will have to consider organizing it into some sort of structure. This is so you, your employees, and sometimes your clients, know who is responsible for doing what. The best way to begin your company structure is along the line of responsibilities within the company. If a few employees specialize in a particular aspect of the company information searches, designate them as such. Describe the others as something like "General Searchers." Clerical staff can also be designated in the General Searchers category. You will eventually have to have a marketing and sales section as well. It is a good idea to have an official company organizational chart that everyone can see and know where they fit into the organization.

Introducing middle management is a crucial part of your company expansion. You must choose your middle managers wisely, because you will be delegating company responsibility to them. You must not only make the delegation of authority to these people, but you have to follow through and not interfere. Let the middle managers manage. They may take a while to grow into the job, but when they do, they will be considerable assets to the company. They should also have the respect of the people who work for them, and they will get this if the people see that you have faith in the managers.

A final word about company organization — keep it simple. Don't overdo it and make it too complicated for the size of the company. Try to keep it in a basic, work-related structure and make sure the structure is understood by everyone. Also, try to avoid having people reporting to more than one boss, although in a small company this is often unavoidable.

8. Exiting the Company

The time will come when you leave the company, and give up the running of it to somebody else. You may opt to retire and continue to own the company, but in all likelihood you will sell it and keep the financial equity you built up over the years.

You can ease out gently by offering to continue running the company for a short while, or act as a consultant to advise the new company manager during the early stages of the new ownership. Eventually you will have to give it up and step aside.

The big question about selling a company is, "What is the price?" You can make calculations based on your annual sales, or annual profit, plus the equity in the company, including customer base and good will. There are many books on this subject; however, you should not do the evaluation yourself. There are companies that specialize in this activity, and your accountant can probably recommend one. Do not hesitate to get professional help in establishing a realistic price for your company, because it is your money that is at stake.

There are several options associated with selling a company. The first is a private sale, either to someone or some company you know, or on the open market. Selling it to someone you know is the least complicated. Once you have established a realistic price you can negotiate with the buyer. You can keep the whole process confidential so that your employees or clients do not know about it and cause complications. This is the way it is usually done.

Selling the company on the open market is more complicated because finding a suitable buyer is not easy. Fortunately, there are companies that specialize in the business of selling other companies. Some of them may already have potential buyers lined up who are looking for new acquisitions. These selling companies charge a fee, but it will probably be worth it to have the process done professionally.

Another option is to sell the company to an investor or group of investors, either completely or partially. If you only sell part of it, you will be able to continue to share future profits of the company, which may be a good pension plan. The investors buying the company could actually be a group of your employees. This is not an uncommon occurrence. No matter who the purchasing investors are, they may want you to stay on for a while and help run the company, which is a nice transition into your retirement.

The most difficult option is to take the company public. That is, create shares that are sold to others, either privately or on the public stock exchange. Shares are usually sold to the public for the first time through an underwriter company, which takes a portion of the money raised as its fee. The shares are often first sold to large investment funds, and the investment companies that buy them hope that the shares will pay dividends and increase in value. The shares are eventually traded on the open market with the same hope. This initial public offering activity, or IPO, was the basis of the dot-com rise and fall in the late '90s.

You can gain from the share sale process in two ways. First, some of the money raised in the selling of the shares can be paid to you for the purchase of the company by the new shareholders. This would have to be disclosed beforehand in the prospectus that explains the share offer. Second, you can retain a portion of the shares, which hopefully will pay future dividends or appreciate in value. It can be a very lucrative way for you to exit the company, as many dot-com billionaires and millionaires will attest to.

Business Plan for Military Budget Opportunity Service

1. Business Opportunity

The US military budgets are usually published on the Internet in the February/March time frame each year, and contain information on most US military acquisition plans and research activities. Companies with applicable products or services can identify opportunities from the budgets, and in many cases obtain sufficient information to pursue the prospects. Additional contact information can be obtained with a knowledgeable search of the Internet.

Mr. C has for years researched the US military budgets for several companies, for business opportunities. Mr. C understands the US military acquisition process, and has the expertise to conduct this research, as well as to do additional Internet searches for contact information to enable companies to pursue the opportunities. The research usually uncovers many opportunities for clients. This service should be of interest to many defense-oriented companies.

The benefit of this service to the customers is that it provides them with information to pursue business with the US military. Some of the specific benefits include information about the following:

- Upcoming programs before the Request For Proposal (RFP) or Request For Information (RFI) is issued.

- When a contract is anticipated.

- Project schedule.

- Quantities to be acquired, if applicable.

- Anticipated unit costs, if available.

- Position and/or name of the program or project manager, and the location of the office.

- Name of companies involved in the project, at the R&D level, as previous contractors, or as anticipated sole source.

- Name of key individual with whom to start the business pursuit, with telephone number and/or email address, if available.

2. Deliverables

The list of opportunities that Mr. C would deliver to the client would —

- be aimed at the client's specific product as defined in the proposal and purchase order or contract;

- be aimed at a specific military service as defined in the proposal and purchase order or contract; and

- Provide a list of opportunities found, including —

  - description of the opportunity, and possibly an estimated win probability, if determinable;

  - funding;

- time frame;
- military program/project manager, if available;
- companies involved, if available;
- contacts and contact details, if available; and
- recommended short-term and long-term marketing action.

3. Company Structure

The company will initially be a sole proprietorship. If the business grows sufficiently, consideration will be given to making it an incorporated company. The name of the sole proprietorship will be Military Business Opportunities (MBO).

4. Potential Clients

The Defense Industries of America (DIA) website lists about 1,400 members. These are companies seriously involved in defense business. These will be the initial potential clients, and others may be added as the business grows.

5. Competition

A number of the larger military equipment suppliers will have their own people scanning the military budgets for opportunities, and some of these large companies work with lobbyist companies in Washington who also scan the military budgets. Approximately 15 percent of the DIA companies are branches of large military equipment companies, and would probably not be interested in the service of MBO.

Many smaller companies who are members of DIA only provide components to larger companies, and as such would not be interested in bidding on military projects directly. Approximately 30 percent of the DIA member companies are in this category, and are probably not interested in the MBO service.

The indirect competition, that is, companies who want to do the budget searches themselves even though they do not have the time for it, are estimated to be about 60 percent of the eligible companies listed by DIA.

6. Market Share of Clients

Of the 1,400 potential clients, approximately 15 percent are large companies who will probably not be interested in MBO. This reduces the 1,400 down to 1,190. Similarly, approximately 30 percent of the 1,400 listed companies are small component suppliers probably not interested in MBO, reducing the number by 420 to 770. Finally, of this remaining number, about 60 percent will want to do the work themselves and not be interested in contracting MBO. Thus the market share of clients would be approximately 308.

It is assumed that the 308 clients will have to be obtained over a five-year build up, and the annual numbers can only be estimated. Assume about half of the contracted clients would stay with MBO from year to year, with the other half opting for only a one time contract. The number of clients estimated for each of the first five years is as follows:

Year 1   24 clients

Year 2   36 clients

Year 3   50 clients

SELF-COUNSEL PRESS — START & RUN AN INTERNET RESEARCH BUSINESS 08

Year 4   80 clients

Year 5   118 clients

7.   Marketing Procedure

The marketing procedure will be in two thrusts:

- Create an Internet site that advertises the service and allows potential clients to request a proposal directly via the Internet. Work to have the site come up high on search engines.

- Direct mail: Identify suitable companies to target from various databases including the DIA website. Obtain the potential client's interest through direct mail to the head of marketing, either by email or by postal mail. Include a form for the client to complete and fax to MBO, with details of product, so MBO can return a proposal. Also invite the potential client to request more information by telephone or email.

8.   Sales Procedure

The sales procedure to obtain a contract or purchase order from the potential client is as follows:

- If the potential client requests more info, contact him or her by telephone or email with a sales pitch, and gauge the seriousness of the client's interest. Encourage the client to complete and send in the MBO website request for proposal or the mailed fax form.

- If the potential client returns a completed website request or fax form requesting a proposal, call him or her for more details and gauge the seriousness of the interest.

- Submit a proposal to the potential client, including a not-to-exceed price, and a suggested contracting procedure.

- Follow up in a few weeks if no response to the proposal.

9.   Project Work Procedure

The procedure to carry out the project work for each client-defined product or service, and each applicable military service is as follows. The information in square brackets is an estimate of the number of hours the step would take, assuming the search will be through five of the ten US military budgets.

- For the defined product or service, scan each item in each applicable budget of a defined US military service (i.e., Army, Air Force, Navy, Marines), to identify potential opportunities. The procedure for this step is:

  - Scan the applicable budget index and identify potential items. [Assume 0.1 hour per budget, 5 x 0.1 = 0.5 project hours.]

  - Read the potential item description and make an educated assessment to determine whether to disregard and go on to the next item, or to read further into the item. [Assume 15 items per budget, at 0.05 hours each, 15 x 5 x 0.05 hour = 3.75 project hours.]

  - If the item appears relevant, continue reading other pages of the budget item to obtain as much information as possible. [Assume 10 items per budget, at 0.1 hours each, 10 x 5 x 0.1 hour = 5.0 project hours.]

- For each relevant opportunity, Google with various keywords to confirm or reject the opportunity and, if applicable, to obtain additional information including:

- Additional description information.

- Military program/project manager identity, location, telephone number, and email address.

- Companies probably interested in the program, with information obtained from brochures, news announcements, contact people, and partners.

- [Assume 10 opportunities per budget, and each would take 0.25 hours, 10 x 5 x 0.25 = 12.5 project hours.]

- For each opportunity make a report of available information including:

  - Description of opportunity

  - Funding

  - Schedule

  - Quantities

  - Military program/project manager

  - Companies involved in the R&D level, as previous contractors, or as anticipated sole source.

  - [Assume 10 opportunities in total worth reporting, and each report write-up would take 0.3 hours, 10 x 0.3 = 3.0 project hours.]

- If applicable, assess the win probability as high, medium, or low. [Assume 10 opportunities at 0.05 hours each, 10 x 0.05 = 0.5 project hours.]

- Draft overall report in a standard format with the above information [Assume 1.0 project hour.]

- Make recommendations for the pursuit. [Assume 0.5 project hours.]

The above time estimates total 26.75 hours per project involving five different budgets. If only three budgets are involved, such as the three US Army R&D budgets, the time estimates are reduced to (26.75 x 3/5) 16.05 hours.

10. Working Team

The initial working team will consist of Mr. C alone. It is estimated that over a year he will spend 35 working days on statuary holidays, holidays, and sickness. He will have to spend at least one day a week on company marketing, promotion, and sales, for a total of 52 days a year. Another half a day a week should be allowed for company administration, for an annual total of 26 days. The total non-billable time is thus (35 + 52 + 26) 113 days per year. Considering 260 non-weekend days per year, this leaves (260 - 113) 147 days per year for contracted work. Based on an eight-hour day, this is equivalent to 1,176 hours per year of billable time.

11. Projected Revenue

The estimated time available per year for billable work is 147 days, or 1,176 hours. At a charge-out rate of $90 per hour, this will enable a maximum annual revenue of $105,840. The number of contracted projects required per year to earn this maximum revenue, at an estimated average project time of 25 hours, is 1,176 divided by 25, or about 47.

However, the number of contracts will be considerably lower during the first year, and gradually build in numbers. Based on the annual number of clients estimated in section 6., Market Share of Clients, the estimated revenue for each of the first five years is projected to be as follows in the table below. This is based on an average project of 25 hours, which at $90 per hour would be $2,250.

Year 1	24 client projects	$54,000
Year 2	36 client projects	$81,000
Year 3	50 client projects	$112,500
Year 4	80 client projects	$180,000
Year 5	118 client projects	$265,500

If the market share estimates are correct, and since a one-person company can only handle about 47 client projects a year, the company will have to expand in the third year of operation. This future expansion is dealt with in section 15.

12. Projected Expenses

The projected expenses can be worked out for each contracted client project. These costs can be divided into the following categories.

- Personnel

  The initial personnel expense will be the owner's salary. Consider this to be $60,000 per year, or $5,000 per month.

- Website

  Assume the cost of a professional to design and upload the website to be $700, and an additional $200 to maximize search engine hits, for a total of $900. Assume the cost of hosting the website to be $40 per month, or $480 per year. The first year website expense is (900 + 480) $1,380, and in subsequent years it is $480.

- Marketing and sales costs

  Assume that only 15 percent of the companies contacted by mail will respond with a request for further information or proposal, and that only a third of those receiving a proposal will contract, making the contracted response 5 percent or 1 in 20. To send out the 20 initial letters would cost (20 x $1) $20 per eventual client, and to send the proposals would cost (3 x $2) $6, for a total marketing cost of $26 per client.

  The time to obtain a client would be about 1 hour for the initial mailing, about (3 x 1.5) 4.5 hours for the three proposals, and about 0.5 hrs for follow up, for a total of 6 hours per client.

- Delivery cost

  The cost of delivering the report would be about $10.

  The time to complete the work for each client, as stated in section 11., would be about 25 hours.

- Office overhead costs

  Assume Internet costs of (12 x $51) $612 per year, computer equipment amortization of ($2000 x 30%) $600 per year, and miscellaneous office expenses of (12 x $30) $360 per year, for a total of $1,572.

13. Profit/Loss Analysis

The profit and loss analysis of the company over the first five years is shown in the following table. The numbers are based on the previously projected revenue and expenses, as well as the future expansion considerations discussed in section 15.

	Year 1	Year 2	Year 3	Year 4	Year 5
Projected Client Projects	24	36	50	80	118
Projected Revenue	54,000	81,000	112,500	180,000	265,500
Projected Expenses					
Personnel	60,000	60,000	60,000	60,000	60,000
Contracted help			43,750	81,250	128,750
Website	1,380	480	480	480	480
Marketing & sales	624	936	1,300	2,080	3,068
Delivery	240	360	500	800	1,118
Office	1,572	1,572	1,572	1,572	1,572
Total expenses	63,816	63,348	107,602	146,182	194,988
Profit or Loss (-)	**(9,816)**	**17,652**	**4,898**	**33,818**	**70,512**
*Assume contracted help in years 3, 4, and 5 at $50 per hour, or $1,250 per 25-hour contract. **Assume the company principal devoting more time to marketing and sales, and thus working on only 15 client contracts per year in years 3, 4, and 5, with the rest being done by contracted help.					

14. Financing

The profit/loss analysis indicates a loss in the first year that will have to be covered by external financing. This will be done by a bank line of credit arrangement for the company, and failing that, a bank personal line of credit arrangement set up by the owner.

15. Future Expansion

The market share projections indicate that the company could take on extra business if the manpower was available. It may be possible to acquire this extra manpower, but is should be on the following basis:

- All work will be on the basis of a contract for each project, at a fixed price based on $50 per hour.

- The contracted help will be given the methodology and budget information, but will have to provide his or her own office and computer support.

- The contracted help will have to sign a nondisclosure agreement and a non-compete agreement.

16. Action Time Line

The first step in getting the MBO business is to find a suitable website designer and get the website up and running. While the website is being designed and launched, work on the direct-mail marketing. This will require the following time line:

Action	Date
Identify a suitable website designer	August 2009
Have the website deigned	August to October 2009
Launch the website	October 2009
Identify the first 20 companies to target	September 2009
Draft suitable marketing letter & RFP form	September 2009
Produce marketing letters & RFP	September 2009
Initial mailing	October 2009
Draft suitable proposal format	October 2009
Monthly mailings (thereafter), beginning in	November 2009

APPENDIX B

ABC Research Services
1234 Main Street, Anywhere, NY 123456
Tel: 800-555-1234

March 20, 2009

William Richards
Fabulous Cosmetics
789 Some Street
Sometown, NY 24680

Dear Mr. Richards:

1. This letter will confirm the arrangements made between ABC Research Services (herein called ABC) and FABULOUS COSMETICS, whereby ABC has agreed to provide FABULOUS COSMETICS with research services relating to the expansion of the ABC cosmetic products business. The tasks that ABC may do for FABULOUS COSMETICS include:

    a. Identifying international competitors of the FABULOUS COSMETICS products.

    b. Identifying possible international marketing agents and distributors for FABULOUS COSMETICS.

    c. Identifying suitable trade shows.

    d. Identifying federal and state government assistance for marketing, research and development, and other activities.

    e. Other related activities as agreed by both parties.

2. Prior to conducting any work on a FABULOUS COSMETICS project, ABC will provide FABULOUS COSMETICS with an estimate of the time and cost of the project work. ABC will not begin work on a FABULOUS COSMETICS project until receiving approval from an authorized representative of FABULOUS COSMETICS.

3. FABULOUS COSMETICS will compensate ABC for the services provided with hourly rate payments of $85 per hour. These payments shall be made at the end of each month by FABULOUS COSMETICS to ABC, following a detailed invoice provided by ABC to FABULOUS COSMETICS, unless otherwise agreed by both parties. The rate shall be reviewed annually and amended as agreed by both parties.

4. FABULOUS COSMETICS will reimburse ABC for reasonable travel, living, and other expenses ABC may incur in providing the services under this agreement, but these expenses must be approved by FABULOUS COSMETICS prior to their occurrence.

5. With respect to all information supplied by FABULOUS COSMETICS to ABC, other than information available to the general public, ABC will keep all such information confidential, and notwithstanding the expiration or termination of this agreement, ABC will not disclose such information to any person outside FABULOUS COSMETICS or ABC at any time without the prior permission of FABULOUS COSMETICS to do so.

6. This agreement shall extend for a period of two (2) years commencing on 20 March, 2009, and will automatically renew annually thereafter on the anniversary of the contract unless terminated by either party. The agreement may be terminated by either party at any time by giving the other party not less than thirty (30) days prior notice.

7. This agreement shall be deemed to be a contract made under the laws of the state of New York, and for all purposes it shall be construed in accordance with and governed by these laws.

8. If the foregoing paragraphs correctly set forth your understanding of the arrangements now agreed upon between FABULOUS COSMETICS and ABC, please sign two copies of this letter and mail one of them to ABC at the above postal address.

Yours truly,

I. M. Good, President
ABC Research Services

UNDERSTOOD AND AGREED

For: FABULOUS COSMETICS

By: _____

        William Richards

CONTRACT EFFECTIVE AS OF JANUARY 06, 2009

BETWEEN: TEACH YOURSELF INC, an incorporated company with head office at 4321 White Street, Hometown, MS
(in this agreement called "TEACH")

AND: ABC Research Services, with head office at 1234 Main street, Anywhere, NY
(in this agreement called "ABC")

WHEREAS:

A. TEACH has computer based training products that it desires to further develop and market;

B. ABC provides information research services; and

C. because of ABC's information research services, and the requirements of TEACH to develop and market its products, TEACH and ABC wish to enter into a contract.

NOW THEREFORE the parties agree as follows:

1. TEACH and ABC shall be conclusively deemed to have agreed that the foregoing recitals are true and correct in each and every respect.

2. The ABC information research activities may include the following:

    a) Researching the market for competitive products or services.

    b) Identifying new developments in computer-based training.

    c) Researching new markets for the TEACH products and services.

    d) Other related activities as agreed by both parties.

3. TEACH will compensate ABC for its research activities at the rate of $85 per hour, and TEACH will pay ABC for all expenses associated with the activities. The compensation will be paid to ABC by TEACH within 30 days of ABC submitting an invoice for its services. ABC will only charge for activities approved by TEACH.

4. TEACH will provide suitable service and product information to ABC.

5. ABC acknowledges that in order to properly provide services to TEACH it will have to have access to TEACH product, development, customer, and marketing information. ABC accordingly agrees to treat as confidential, all knowledge and documentation which is acquired during the course of providing services to TEACH, both present and in the future, and agrees that all of the foregoing shall be and shall remain the property of TEACH. ABC shall not, during the course of providing services in accordance with this contract with TEACH, or at any time thereafter, directly or indirectly, divulge to any person, firm, or corporation the confidential knowledge and documentation of TEACH.

6. This agreement will be in effect for a period of two (2) years from the contract effective date, and will automatically renew annually thereafter on the anniversary of the contract effective date unless terminated by either party.

7. The agreement may be terminated by either party at any time by informing the other party in writing giving ninety (90) days notice.

8. All of the clauses of this agreement are severable from each other and will survive the invalidity of any other clause of this agreement.

9. This agreement shall be read with all changes in gender and/or number that may reasonably be required by the context and shall be interpreted in accordance with the laws of the state of New York.

DATED AT ANYWHERE NY THIS _____ DAY OF _____, 20_____

SIGNED, SEALED, AND DELIVERED)
In the presence of)
) TEACH YOURSELF INC.
)
)
) _____
) John Knowledge, President
) I have the authority to bind the
) corporation
)
)
)
) ABC Research Services
)
)
) _____
) I.M. Good, President
Witness to the signatures) I have the authority to bind the
) company

Proposal To

Fabulous Cosmetics

To

Provide Research Services

(Dated 20 March, 2009)

1. ABC Understanding of Requirement

ABC Research Services' understanding of the Fabulous Cosmetics situation is as follows:

- Fabulous Cosmetics manufactures and markets a line of natural, holistic beauty products. The company has been in business since 2001, and current annual sales are in the $1,000,000 range.

- The majority of Fabulous Cosmetics sales are through the website, and these are mainly to US customers.

- Fabulous Cosmetics has attempted to expand into the international market with mixed results.

- Fabulous Cosmetics would like to grow the business in the most cost-effective way.

2. Objectives

The ABC objective of this agreement is to provide Fabulous Cosmetics with information to enable the most cost-effective way to grow the Fabulous Cosmetics business.

3. Statement of Work

To obtain and provide the relevant information to Fabulous Cosmetics, ABC will carry out each assigned task in approximately the following ways:

- Learn more about the current Fabulous Cosmetics products, marketing methods, customer profiles, and customer purchasing trends. This will be done by studying the website information, by reading marketing brochures, and by telephone interview of the Fabulous Cosmetics management at a time convenient to them.

- Carry out the needed research to obtain the relevant information.

- Assess the obtained information and arrange it in an easily understood format.

- Provide Fabulous Cosmetics with a report on the above activity.

4. Deliverables

On the completion of a task ABC will deliver a report that will—

- provide the requested information;

- assess the information, if applicable; and

- propose follow-on work, if warranted.

5. Follow-on Work

ABC will provide Fabulous Cosmetics with recommendations for follow-on work, including an estimate of the work and costs involved. However, ABC will not undertake the work without the approval of Fabulous Cosmetics.

6. Price and Schedule

Prior to conducting any work on a Fabulous Cosmetics project, ABC will provide Fabulous Cosmetics with an estimate of the time and cost of the project work. ABC will not begin the work until authorized by Fabulous Cosmetics. Fabulous Cosmetics will compensate ABC for the services provided with hourly rate payments of $85 per hour. These payments shall be made at the end of each month by Fabulous Cosmetics to ABC, following a detailed invoice provided by ABC to Fabulous Cosmetics, unless otherwise agreed by both parties. The rate shall be reviewed annually and amended as agreed by both parties.

The schedule for each task will be proposed to Fabulous Cosmetics along with the task and cost estimate.

7. Confidentiality

With respect to all information supplied to or acquired by ABC during the course of the proposed work, other than information available to the general public, ABC will keep all such information confidential and, notwithstanding the expiration or termination of the contract, ABC will not disclose such information to any person outside Fabulous Cosmetics at any time without the company's prior written permission to do so.

8. ABC Systems Limited

ABC Systems Limited has been providing client companies with information research services since 1994. Client companies have varied in size from large multinationals to very small start-ups. Some previous and current ABC clients include:

- Heating Systems Inc.

- Boston Design

- Computing Equipment Inc.

- HFL Manufacturing Ltd.

- Mountain Ridge Communications

- News Publishers Inc.

- Scanning Industries Inc.

- West Wind Corporation

APPENDIX E

The following is a sample request for proposal page you could have your website designer develop and include on your website. The interested client completes the information, and when the client hits a "Submit" button, the request is automatically emailed to your email address.

Request for Proposal

Please send us a proposal to provide a monthly report on construction technology changes in the following areas. (Please check those you are interested in.)

☐ Techniques

☐ Materials

☐ Equipment

☐ Tooling

☐ Building codes

I am specifically interested in the following aspects of the industry: *(Complete only if desired.)*

Please send the proposal to:

Name: _____ Position: _____

Company: _____

Postal Address: _____

_____

_____

Email Address: _____

Telephone: _____ Fax: _____

Website: _____

Website Information Request

The following is a suggested information request page you could have your website designer develop and include on your website. The interested client completes the information, and when the client hits a "Submit" button the request is automatically emailed to your email address.

Information Request

Please send me more information about your Internet research service.

Name: _____

Company: _____

Company Position: _____

Company Address: _____

_____

_____

_____

Telephone: _____

Email Address: _____

Website: _____

CONTRACT EFFECTIVE AS OF SEPTEMBER 3, 2009

BETWEEN: OTHERWISE INC., an incorporated company with head office at 427 Mud Street, Hoggtown, NY
(in this agreement called "OINC")

AND: ABC Research Services, with head office at 1234 Main Street, Anywhere, NY
(in this agreement called "ABC")

WHEREAS:

A.   OINC has developed, and currently manufactures and markets, a Hog Transporter that is used to restrain and transport an arousing hog during the artificial insemination of sows, and OINC desires to further increase the sales of this remotely controlled Hog Transporter;

B.   ABC provides information research services; and

C.   because of ABC's information research services, and the requirements of OINC to develop and market its products, OINC and ABC wish to enter into a contract.

NOW THEREFORE the parties agree as follows:

1.   OINC and ABC shall be conclusively deemed to have agreed that the foregoing recitals are true and correct in each and every respect.

2.   ABC will research the international market for the Hog Transporter product, and provide OINC with a report that includes the following:

   a)   The extent of the hog raising industry in North America, Asia, and Europe.

   b)   Areas that have large hog farms in excess of 2,000 sows.

   c)   Names of the large hog farms and contact information.

   d)   Recommended priority of cost-effectively addressing these markets.

3.   ABC will conduct the research and deliver the report to OINC within 90 working days of the date of this agreement.

4.   OINC will compensate ABC for this research and report at the rate of $110 per hour, to a maximum of $5,000.

5.   OINC will provide suitable product information to ABC on the Hog Transporter.

6. ABC acknowledges that in order to properly provide services to OINC it will have to have access to OINC product, development, customer, and marketing information. ABC accordingly agrees to treat as confidential, all knowledge and documentation which is acquired during the course of providing services to OINC, both present and in the future, and agrees that all of the foregoing shall be and shall remain the property of OINC. ABC shall not, during the course of providing services in accordance with this contract with OINC, or at any time thereafter, directly or indirectly, divulge to any person, firm, or corporation the confidential knowledge and documentation of OINC.

7. All of the clauses of this agreement are severable from each other and will survive the invalidity of any other clause of this agreement.

8. This agreement shall be read with all changes in gender and/or number that may reasonably be required by the context and shall be interpreted in accordance with the laws of the state of New York.

DATED AT ANYWHERE, NY THIS _____ DAY OF _____, 20_____

SIGNED, SEALED, AND DELIVERED	) for
In the presence of	) OTHERWISE INC.
	)
	) _____
	) Stanley Farmer, President
	) I have the authority to bind the corporation
	)
	)
	) for
	) ABC Research Services
	)
_____	) _____
Witness to the signatures	) I. M. Good, President
	) I have the authority to bind the company

APPENDIX G

CONTRACT EFFECTIVE AS OF SEPTEMBER 2, 2009

BETWEEN: ELECTRONIC MANUFACTURING INC., an incorporated company with head office at 789 Black Street, Newtown, NY (in this agreement called "EMI")

AND: ABC Research Services, with head office at 1234 Main Street, Anywhere, NY (in this agreement called "ABC")

WHEREAS:

A. EMI designs, develops, and manufactures light emitting diode displays for underwater applications, that it desires to further develop and market;

B. ABC provides information research services; and

C. because of ABC's information research services, and the requirements of EMI to develop and market its products, EMI and ABC wish to enter into a contract.

NOW THEREFORE the parties agree as follows:

1. EMI and ABC shall be conclusively deemed to have agreed that the foregoing recitals are true and correct in each and every respect.

2. The ABC information research activities may include the following:

   a) Researching the market for competitive products.

   b) Identifying new developments in underwater displays and display applications.

   c) Researching new markets for the EMI products and services.

   d) Other related activities as agreed by both parties.

3. EMI will compensate ABC for its research activities at the rate of $85 per hour, and EMI will pay ABC for all expenses associated with the activities. The compensation will be paid to ABC by EMI within 30 days of ABC submitting an invoice for its services. ABC will only charge for activities approved by EMI.

4. EMI requires ABC to respond quickly to EMI tasking. To compensate ABC for providing a rapid response on a continuous basis, EMI will pay ABC a minimum of one thousand dollars ($1,000) per month retainer fee, whether or not ABC does any work for EMI. Monthly compensation for approved activities, as defined in paragraph 3 above, will reduce the $1,000 monthly retainer fee.

5. EMI will designate a person who is authorized to task ABC to conduct specific activities. The tasking may be verbally, by telephone, or by email.

6. EMI will provide suitable service and product information to ABC.

7. ABC acknowledges that in order to properly provide services to EMI it will have to have access to EMI product, development, customer, and marketing information. ABC accordingly agrees to treat as confidential, all knowledge and documentation which is acquired during the course of providing services to EMI, both present and in the future, and agrees that all of the foregoing shall be and shall remain the property of EMI. ABC shall not, during the course of providing services in accordance with this contract with EMI, or at any time thereafter, directly or indirectly, divulge to any person, firm, or corporation the confidential knowledge and documentation of EMI.

8. This agreement will be in effect for a period of two (2) years from the contract effective date, and will automatically renew annually thereafter on the anniversary of the contract effective date unless terminated by either party.

9. The agreement may be terminated by either party at any time by informing the other party in writing giving ninety (90) days notice.

10. All of the clauses of this agreement are severable from each other and will survive the invalidity of any other clause of this agreement.

11. This agreement shall be read with all changes in gender and/or number that may reasonably be required by the context and shall be interpreted in accordance with the laws of the state of New York.

DATED AT ANYWHERE, NY THIS _____ DAY OF _____, 20_____

SIGNED, SEALED, AND DELIVERED	)	for
In the presence of	)	ELECTRONIC MANUFACTURING INC.
	)	_____
	)	William Sharp, President
	)	I have the authority to bind the corporation
	)	
	)	for
	)	ABC Research Services
	)	
_____	)	_____
Witness to the signatures	)	I. M. Good, President
	)	I have the authority to bind the company

Suitable Asian Distributors and/or Agents

for the

Fabulous Cosmetics Products

September 2009

1.   Executive Summary

This investigation identified two companies who could be suitable distributors and/or agents of the Fabulous Cosmetics products. The companies are listed in sections **4.** and **5.** below, together with their contact particulars and a brief description. The most highly recommended company is Asian Cosmetics PLC, with head office in Singapore, and branch offices in Tokyo and Hong Kong. One additional company has been identified in "most promising opportunities." In addition, one company has been identified as an "other" opportunity.

It is recommended that Fabulous Cosmetics contact Asian Cosmetics PLC as soon as possible to negotiate a business arrangement. Failing a deal with Asian Cosmetics PLC, the other most promising opportunity should be contacted, followed by the company listed as other opportunity.

2.   Research Parameters

This project was to identify suitable distributors and/or agents for the Fabulous Cosmetics line of products. The research was to be limited to Southeast Asian, for the following:

- Distributors who would purchase the products from Fabulous Cosmetics in large quantities, stock them, and resell them to retailers.

- Agents, who would arrange for retailers to purchase the products directly from Fabulous Cosmetics.

- Companies that manufactured their own cosmetics and distributed them were to be specifically avoided.

3.   Countries Investigated

More than 200 companies were investigated, in the following countries, as listed in the contract:

- Japan
- Korea
- China
- Thailand
- Malaysia
- Singapore

4. Most Promising Opportunities

The two companies offering the most promising opportunities are listed below with their contact particulars:

1. Asian Cosmetics PLC, 256 Orchard Street, Singapore. The contact is Walter Chew, the new business development manager. His telephone number is 555-123-4567. His email address is chew@asiancosmetics.com. The company website is at asiancosmetics.com. The company distributes a large line of cosmetics throughout Southeast Asia, with branch offices in Tokyo and Hong Kong. It claims gross sales of more than $100 million US dollars per year, which indicates a large and successful company.

2. New China Cosmetics, 123 Cosmetics Street, Malaysia. The contact is Angie Li, the business development manager. Her telephone number is 555-444-9999. Her email address is li@newchinacosmetics.com. The company website is newchinacosmetics.com. The company distributes a line of cosmetics throughout Southeast Asia and has a branch office in Hong Kong. It claims gross sales of more than $75 million US dollars per year, which also indicates a large and successful company.

(You may have more than two companies to list in this section. If so, list the additional companies and their relevant information.)

5. Other Opportunity

The following company may also be suitable as a distributor or agent for Fabulous Cosmetics.

1. Rising Sun Cosmetics, 111 Sun Street, Thailand. The contact is Bob Trinh, the business development manager. His telephone number is 555-555-4499. His email address trinh@risingsuncosmetics.com. The company website is risingsuncosmetics.com. The company distributes a line of cosmetics throughout Southeast Asia. It claims gross sales of more than $50 million US dollars per year.

(You may have more than one company to list in this section. If so, list the additional companies and their relevant information.)

6. Conclusions

This project identified three suitable distributors and/or agents available throughout the targeted Asian countries. Some are more suitable than others as explained in sections **4.** and **5.** Those identified should be interested in a business arrangement with Fabulous Cosmetics.

7. Recommendations

Based on the information obtained and reported, the following recommendations are made:

1. Contact Asian Cosmetics PLC as soon as possible and investigate the possibility of negotiating a business arrangement.

2. If it is not possible to obtain an arrangement with Asian Cosmetics PLC, contact the other most promising opportunity listed in section **4.**

3. If it is still not possible to obtain a suitable business arrangement, contact the company listed as other opportunity in section **5.**

APPENDIX I

ABC Research Services
1234 Main Street, Anywhere, NY 23456
Tel: 800-555-1234

September 4, 2009

James Digger
648 Hope Street
Villagetown, NY 86742

Dear Mr. Digger:

1. This letter will confirm the arrangements made between ABC Research Services (herein called ABC) and yourself, whereby you have agreed to provide ABC with research services when tasked by ABC. The tasks that you may be asked to do by ABC will primarily be information searches on the Internet relating to ABC client contracts.

2. Prior to conducting any work on a project, you will provide ABC with an estimate of the time and cost of the project work outlined to you by ABC. ABC will either accept your estimate and authorize you to do the work, or will further negotiate the arrangement.

3. ABC will compensate you for the services provided with hourly rate payments of $45 per hour. These payments shall be made at the end of each month by ABC to you following a detailed invoice provided to ABC by yourself. The rate shall be reviewed annually and amended as agreed by both parties.

4. ABC will reimburse you for reasonable travel, living, and other expenses you may incur in providing the services under this agreement, but these expenses must be approved by ABC prior to their occurrence.

5. With respect to all information supplied by ABC and its clients to you, other than information available to the general public, you will keep all such information confidential, and notwithstanding the expiration or termination of this agreement, you will not disclose such information to any person outside ABC at any time without the prior permission of ABC to do so.

6. You will be prohibited from working with an ABC competitor, or starting your own business in competition to ABC, for a period of two (2) years after the expiry of this agreement.

7. This agreement shall extend for a period of two (2) years commencing on 4 September, 2009 and will automatically renew annually thereafter on the anniversary of the contract unless terminated by either party. The agreement may be terminated by either party at any time by giving the other party not less than thirty (30) days prior notice.

8. This agreement shall be deemed to be a contract made under the laws of the state of New York, and for all purposes it shall be construed in accordance with and governed by these laws.

9. If the foregoing paragraphs correctly set forth your understanding of the arrangements now agreed upon between yourself and ABC, please sign two copies of this letter and mail one of them to ABC at the postal address listed at the beginning of this document.

Yours truly,

I. M. Good, President
ABC Research Services

UNDERSTOOD AND AGREED

By: _____
         James Digger